Life al Dente

Also by Gina Cascone

Pagan Babies and Other Catholic Memories

Life al Dente

*Laughter and Love in an
Italian-American Family*

❧

Gina Cascone

ATRIA BOOKS

New York   London   Toronto   Sydney   Singapore

ATRIA BOOKS
1230 Avenue of the Americas
New York, NY 10020

ISBN: 978-1-4391-8376-2

First Atria Books hardcover edition July 2003

10 9 8 7 6 5 4 3 2 1

ATRIA BOOKS is a registered trademark of Simon & Schuster, Inc.

Manufactured in the United States of America

For information regarding special discounts for bulk purchases,
please contact Simon & Schuster Special Sales at 1-800-456-6798
or business@simonandschuster.com

For Pietro Paulo Cascone,
My Grandfather,
Who gave me the heart to keep rebuilding in the foothills
of the volcano, because the view is worth it.

Pietro Paulo Cascone

The Great Love of My Life

Contents

Life al Dente

Chapter 1

≈

One of the Boys

I WAS THE firstborn, the son my father always wanted. And so he started almost immediately to mold me into his own image and likeness. For the most part, his efforts were successful. Unfortunately, there was one obstacle, which he could neither overcome nor accept. I was a girl.

My father's first words to my mother after visiting the nursery shortly after my birth were, "It looks like a monkey." Who was he kidding? If I'd had a blue blanket wrapped around me, I could have been a monkey and he would have been too delirious with joy to have noticed.

Still, son or not, I was his kid. "I guess we'll keep it," he nobly announced to my mother after the next visit.

Having thus committed himself, my father tried as hard as he could to protect me from the ugly truth of my genetic makeup for as long as he could. Maybe he even managed to convince himself that it wasn't so. Parents do tend to be blind to their children's shortcomings. And in an Italian family, few things are a greater handicap than being born female.

In the early years, I didn't suffer from it at all. My father worked double-time to turn me into a real man. He taught me not to cry "like a girl"; throw a ball underhand, "like a sissy"; or slap—"if you're going to hit somebody, you punch him." I learned that the secret of winning an argument was turning up the volume of your voice and gesticulating furiously. And I learned to say *vaffanculo* when I was angry.

My mother stood by and let my father have his way as far as my upbringing was concerned. There were two reasons for this. First of all, my mother always let my father have his way. He was her most spoiled child. And secondly, she agreed with him. She wanted me to be strong, quick, and competitive—not the son she'd always wanted but the daughter she'd always wanted.

But sooner or later the horrible truth had to catch up with me and have a real impact on my life. Neither of my parents prepared me for that day. I suppose they meant to and just kept putting it off until it was too late. It certainly would have been easier hearing it from them than from Little Nicky Santucci.

Little Nicky ran the neighborhood—insofar as all activities regarding us kids were concerned. He was, for all intents and purposes, the self-proclaimed mayor of Melrose Avenue. It was a tight little street. The houses and their inhabitants were packed close together. There were maybe half a dozen single-family homes on our block. Most of us lived in semidetached or row houses.

Nicky lived in what was by far the biggest house on the corner of the block. It was white stucco with a walled-in patio and garden. A flower shop occupied the front half of the ground floor.

Nicky's father, Big Nick, ran the flower shop. He owned it actually. Big Nick did not look like the kind of guy who would be much interested in flowers; but then, Michelangelo didn't look like the kind of guy whose soul drove him to create such great beauty. So who knew? The difference was that I'd never actually seen Big Nick touch a flower, except to snap off its stem and stick the bud into the lapel of his jacket. And while it was pretty clear that everybody thought that being a florist was kind of a sissy job, I never heard anybody tease Big Nick about it, or about anything else for that matter. So I never did either. Besides, Big Nick was always real nice to us kids. He liked to pass out candy and, on special occasions, even dollar bills.

Little Nicky, on the other hand, did not seem to have inherited his father's magnanimous nature. Little Nicky was a loose cannon with a short fuse. You never knew what he was going to do next. Half the time he didn't know either. So being able to play with Nicky was a real test of one's mettle.

One of his favorite gags was dropping his frog, Nunzio, down someone's shirt. Carla Moretti was really the only one who panicked more than neurotic, little Nunzio. Then there was the time that Nicky ate a night crawler and Crazy Carla threw up. I have to admit, it took real intestinal fortitude on my part to keep my dinner down through that one. I just kept smiling and swallowing. I would not give Nicky the satisfaction of seeing me crack. That was his game after all. Nothing gave him greater pleasure than knowing that he'd found someone's breaking point.

But it was one day when he wasn't even trying that he finally found mine.

It was a perfect summer day right after fourth grade. I'd decided I was in the mood for a baseball game. So I got my glove and headed for Nicky's house. All baseball games, like everything else that went on in the neighborhood, were organized through Nicky. I went through the garden gate, around back to the family entrance, and rang the bell.

Nicky opened the door, took one look at me, and practically slammed the door in my face.

"Hey!" I pushed back.

"Go away," he told me.

I stuck my foot in the door like an unwanted salesman. "What's wrong with you?"

"I can't play with you anymore," he told me through the crack in the doorway.

I snickered. "What did you do now?" I prodded, thinking that his mother had grounded him again.

"Nothing," he said defensively.

"Then why can't you play?"

"I just can't, okay?"

"No, it's not okay," I told him. "I'm not going away until you tell me why."

"Because the guys are here."

I didn't see the problem. "Great! Let's go to the empty lot and play ball."

"That's what we were going to do."

"Well then, let's go," I insisted.

"You're not invited."

"Says who?"

"Everybody."

"Why?"

"Because you're a girl. You have cooties."

"You're a human cootie and we all play with you."

"Good thing you're a girl, or I'd beat you up."

"Why don't you come out here and try it." I put up my fists, left one high to protect my face.

"I don't hit girls," he said, condescendingly.

"Since when?" He'd rid me of a "baby" molar two weeks earlier when I'd dropped my left. The tooth fairy brought me a dollar and a quarter for that tooth. A quarter from my mother, who told me that the tooth fairy really wouldn't think that I deserved anything for losing a tooth in a fight. And a buck from the old man, who was glowing with pride.

"I don't hit girls," he reiterated, even more solicitously. "And I don't play with them. Face it, you're a girl and you have cooties."

I stood there dumbfounded. What else could I do? I wasn't allowed to cry. And Nicky wouldn't come out into the open where I could get a good shot at him.

When I finally turned to leave, Nicky slammed the door behind me. I walked away from the house, fighting to maintain my composure. When I got around to the front of the house, out on the pavement where I was pretty sure Nicky wouldn't be able to see me, I started to run for home. I heard myself panting as I ran and I heard a few whimpers escape. Rejected by Little Nicky Santucci! What worse indignities could one be forced to suffer in this life?

When I got home, my mother was in the kitchen so I managed to sneak past her. I went upstairs where I could be alone in my misery. All the frustration and rage I felt came pouring out. In no time at all, I was climbing the walls. I was literally climbing the walls. I did that to relieve pressure.

There was a section of hallway upstairs that was long and narrow, and when I braced myself with one hand and one foot against each wall, I could shimmy up. Then I could pace the hallway up near the ceiling. The trick was turning around. It was best to do that at the end of the hallway so that there was the third wall—over the door, of course—to use for balance.

One small slip and I'd fall to the floor. I wasn't afraid of the distance of the fall. But I didn't like to fall in the hallway because it made a huge thud that my mother could hear downstairs, and she would know what I was doing. Not that the footprints I left on the walls weren't a dead giveaway.

I was careful as I walked back and forth and up and down the walls thinking about what Nicky had said. "Face it, you're a girl."

So what? I thought. Why did that matter? I was one of the best baseball players in the neighborhood and now they weren't going to let me play because I was a girl! Why did being a girl make a difference all of a sudden? It had never mattered before.

The more I thought about it, the more it came clear to me that it had always mattered. I should have seen it. But I didn't. Or maybe I wouldn't. It was always there though. When my father would come in when I was playing with Nicky, he'd say, "Hey, Butch, how's it going?" to Nicky. "Butch!" He always called Nicky "Butch." He called me "Chicken."

My parents' friends and relatives were always squeezing me and pinching my cheeks and telling me how cute I was. Nobody ever gushed all over Nicky, telling him how cute he was. Understandably. Still, you would think that just to be polite, somebody could lie. But Nicky wasn't expected to be cute. Not just because he was Nicky, but also because he was a boy.

Boys weren't expected to be much of anything. And they got away with murder because of it. "Boys will be boys." That's what they all said when Nicky got kicked out of Catholic school. That's what they said the time he got stuck in the sewer when he'd jumped in after Nunzio. That's what they said when he got dirty or tore his clothes or broke something. One lousy smack and "boys will be boys," that was all that ever happened to Nicky. One step out of line and I got lectured and plunked in a chair for an hour to "think about it."

Well I was sure thinking about it now.

"Hey." A voice from behind startled me. I hadn't heard anybody come up the stairs. Instinctively, I jumped to the floor and turned around, only to see my father smiling. "You'd better not let your mother catch you doing that," he warned. "Let me see how you get up there."

"Nah, I'm not in the mood anymore. Besides, Mommy will probably come up and catch me."

"No she won't. I'll look out for her." My father loved to be my partner in crime.

"I don't feel like it," I moped.

"Come on," he cajoled. "Give you a buck if you show me how you do it." That was another thing my father taught me—never pass up an opportunity to make a buck. I braced myself and went straight up to the ceiling. When I got there, I reached out my hand. My father dug into his pocket and peeled a bill off the roll he always carried and handed it to me. I took it and put it in my own pocket.

"That's great!" He laughed. "How did you figure out you could do that?"

I shrugged.

He finally caught on to my mood. "What's the matter, Chicken?"

"Nothin'."

"Come on, tell Daddy what's wrong."

"I hate boys," I said adamantly, looking down at him.

His face dropped. "Why would you hate boys?"

The disappointment in his voice put me on the defensive. "They won't let me play ball with them. Nicky says it's because I'm a girl." There, I said it! The horrible truth was out.

My father looked more hurt by what happened to me than I was. "Okay," he started calmly. "So you're a girl," he admitted as easily as one might admit to murder. "What else did he say to hurt your feelings?"

"Cooties. He said I have cooties."

"Little Nicky's got a hell of a nerve calling anybody a cootie."

"Yeah. I know. I told him that he was a human cootie."

My father laughed. "Good one," he said, congratulating me for standing up to Nicky. "What did he say to that?"

"Nothing. He still said that nobody wanted to play with me because I'm a girl."

We were back to the main problem, and my father's face reflected the seriousness of it. "Come to Daddy," he said, reaching out his arms to get me down from the ceiling. I jumped and he caught me and carried me into his room. He sat on the bed, cradling me on his lap. Tears were running down my cheeks and dripping off my chin before I let any sound escape. It was all right to cry now. That was one of the rules. You could cry in front of your parents. That was not a show of weakness, but one of love and trust.

"Poor baby," he said, wiping the tears. My father's voice was very deep, and when he used it to comfort, the words weren't important; it was the sound that was soothing, almost hypnotic.

"I don't want to be a girl," I sobbed.

"I know," he said, comforting me, stroking my hair.

"I hate myself for being a girl."

"Oh stop that. Don't say stupid things like that. You just remember that you're smarter and tougher than all of them. You're my baby, so you've got to be. And you're prettier too."

"Being pretty is dumb," I said in a monotone, my head resting on his shoulder.

"No it's not. You're pretty. You're my pretty baby."

"I'm not a baby."

"Yes you are." He laughed. "You are my baby. And you always will be. Even when you're forty years old, you'll still be my baby."

I didn't say anything.

"Don't you want to be my baby?"

"Yeah." I told him what he wanted to hear.

"Promise?"

"I promise."

"And promise me you'll never grow up to be one of those silly ladies."

"What?"

"Don't grow up to be one of those silly ladies, okay?" he repeated.

"Silly ladies like who?"

"Like all of them," he said with authority, sounding frighteningly like Nicky. "Promise me," he said with urgency, looking me right in the eye, his hand holding my chin.

"Okay, Daddy." I nodded. "I promise."

And so began a lifetime of confusion.

≈

Chapter 2

Come Si Chiamas

FROM THE moment I was made to feel that I was some-how less, I was always on the lookout for differences be-tween the sexes and, more importantly, ways in which I could minimize them in myself.

Probably the biggest difference, and the one most trouble-some to me, was balls.

My father only admired people who had a set of balls. I had never seen a set and at first I wasn't even sure what they were or where you'd find them. But I knew my father had a set of his own. I knew that because whenever he came home from a bad day at the office, I'd hear him complain to my mother "my aching balls." I learned that other men had balls too, because whenever my father had someone where he wanted him he'd tell my mother he "had him by the balls."

Even the damn dog had balls. My father refused to allow for him to be neutered, no matter how much my mother argued in favor of it.

"The vet says we really ought to do it," my mother would insist every time the dog escaped from the house or the backyard and she had to chase after him. "It will make him more docile," she would say. "He won't want to run away anymore."

"He won't want to do anything anymore," my father would shoot back. "He'll lose his will to live. Think about it, while all his buddies are sitting around outside, licking their *come si chiamas*, what's he supposed to do?"

Yeah, what's a guy supposed to do without his *come si chiamas*—his whatchamacallits—his balls?

Balls, balls, balls. It seemed to me that men were always calling attention to them. And I couldn't for the life of me understand why. Once I caught a quick glimpse of them up Nicky's baggy bathing suit leg. It was disgusting! It looked like something had died up there. And this was what men made such a fuss about? They worshipped them, treated them like gold, called them the family jewels, and wore them with pride.

Like most things that are priceless, I also found out that balls are quite fragile and must be treated with the utmost care. I learned that fact quite clearly while I was still very young. It was a Sunday afternoon. While my mother was busily cooking and cleaning, my father spent most of the day stretched out on the sofa, watching television. He was supposed to be watching me. I decided that I had gone long enough without attention or affection from him. My most effective attention getter was to jump up onto his lap, something that I'd done countless times before. But on this particular occasion, I'd no sooner landed on my father when he let out a howl like a mortally wounded animal. He rolled over and I fell from the couch, hitting my head on the coffee table. While he groaned, I cried. And for the first time in my life he made no attempt to comfort me. I wailed. He groaned some more.

My mother rushed in from the kitchen and scooped me up from the floor. While she held me, trying to soothe away my tears, she asked my father what had happened. I can remember looking at my father while my mother waited for a response. His eyes were bugged out, his face was red and contorted with pain, and he seemed not to be able to speak.

She asked a second time. "What happened?"

"Your kid tried to kill me, that's what happened," my father growled, holding himself.

Immediately my mother seemed to understand what had occurred and she put her hand to her mouth to stifle a laugh.

"What the hell do women think is so funny about catching a shot in the balls?" My father's pain had turned to anger. "How would you like to get kicked in the balls?"

For some reason, that made my mother laugh even harder.

"And that's why that kid has no respect for me," he snapped.

"Oh come on, it couldn't have been that bad," she said as she took my hand and led me back into the kitchen with her.

But it must have been that bad because from that day on, I was never allowed to jump on him without warning. Moreover, I began to realize that he wasn't the only man who worried about protecting himself. For example, I learned from my father that in boxing you could beat a guy's face until it was pulp. You could knock out teeth or punch his nose right off. But you weren't allowed even one hit below the belt. In addition, my observations led me to understand that not only were they to be protected, but they were also to be pampered, almost to the point where it seemed to become a preoccupation.

At the sidelines of every baseball or football game, what do you see? Guys holding, scratching, or simply rearranging them. And both men and little boys seemed to be perfectly justified in scratching in public. It was acceptable, and everyone seemed to understand why it was necessary. On the other hand, as a girl, I wasn't allowed to scratch anything in public, even a mosquito bite on my arm.

The truth of the matter was that I resented them, resented the fact that they were the most respected, protected, pampered, and talked-about part of the male anatomy. Women had nothing in comparison. It wasn't that men didn't discuss parts of the female anatomy at length. It's just that when they were discussed, it was in whispers. I'd heard my father and his brother, Uncle Gene. Was it supposed to be a compliment when a man noticed that a woman had "great boobs"? Somehow I doubted it. With a set of balls, you could conquer the world. I'd never heard the same said about a set of boobs. And I'd never heard any guy wanting to get himself a set. Who wanted them? Not me, that was for sure.

What I really wanted was what my father and Little Nicky had. It was balls that gave Nicky license to call me a cootie. Nicky had them and my father made a big point about that fact. He'd always say, "That Nicky's one ballsy kid." So Nicky had balls. And I had a problem.

The problem was, like most of my problems, solved by my mother. She taught me that balls were more than an appendage; having them was an attitude.

My father had forgotten their anniversary. Again. For the fifth year in a row. She'd always tried to understand his excuses. He was sorry, but he was busy and had a lot on his mind. And didn't he, after all, work hard every day to make a good life for her? And then he'd promise to make it up to her. And that would be that until the next year.

But her anniversary was important to her. Tough as she could be sometimes, my mother was a hopeless romantic. And for some reason that was often beyond my understanding, she adored my father.

They were a glamorous couple. There was never a time in my life when I didn't look at the two of them together and marvel at how beautiful they were. I always thought that my father looked exactly like Dean Martin. He didn't see it. He thought that he looked like Victor Mature. Whenever he'd say so, my mother was quick to point out that her old boyfriend, Eldin, the one from whom my father had stolen her affections, always told her that she looked like Hedy Lamarr.

Nothing was more comical than watching *Samson and Delilah,* starring Victor Mature and Hedy Lamarr, with my parents. In fact, I don't think I ever actually saw the movie. The real show took place on the sofa in front of the television. It started out as narcissistic posturing. Which one of them really looked like a movie star? Then came the yucky love scene where each one decided that the other was even better looking than any movie star.

Movies were a big part of my parents' lives. They met and fell in love at the movies. He was the head usher and she was the candy girl who sneaked him Chunkys for free. They dated through high school and married a year after they graduated.

My mother gave up a scholarship in journalism and worked as a secretary in order to put my father through school instead. She always put family first and never gave any hint that she regretted that decision.

But the year that my father not only forgot their anniversary, but also went out for drinks with the guys instead of coming home for dinner, my mother decided to teach him a lesson he wouldn't soon forget.

She had the locks on the doors changed.

When he got home, my mother, my baby sister, and I were sitting on the couch watching television. After several unsuccessful attempts to unlock the door, my father started banging on it. My mother made it clear with a wave of her hand that we were to ignore him. Finally, when it became apparent to my father that he wasn't going to get into the house through the door, he tried to break in through the basement window.

That was when my mother called the police. She told them that she was home alone with her children and that there was a prowler outside. A squad car was there in a matter of minutes, lights flashing and siren blaring. This was almost more fun than the pony they'd gotten for my birthday party. I could tell that my mother was enjoying it more.

My father didn't get hauled away because he knew the cops who answered the call. He knew lots of cops because he was a lawyer for the Policemen's Benevolent Association. And because he knew all the cops he didn't enjoy having to explain to them why he was trying to break into his own house while his wife and kids were in there watching television.

The laughter coming from outside told us that the cops were enjoying themselves almost as much as my mother was. They knocked on the door and asked her if she wanted to keep him or have him locked up. My father begged to be locked up. My mother decided to keep him and let him in. While my mother invited the cops in for coffee, my father stormed up to his room and locked himself in, presumably to punish mother. It was always his view when he was angry with her that depriving her of his company was the ultimate torture for her.

When the cops finally left, we went back to watching television as if nothing had happened. We knew full well that my father would be down at any moment. *Gunsmoke* was about to start. He never missed an episode. The night my sister was born, he made my mother wait until it was over before he took her to the hospital. Once I threw up right on the floor, waiting for a commercial to come on so he would finally get me a bucket. He certainly wasn't going to miss his favorite show trying to make a point.

The door to the bedroom squeaked open just as the theme song came on and we heard the footsteps coming down the stairs. When he came into the room, we all looked up at him. My mother was the only one smiling.

"I ought to kill you," he said in a low, controlled voice that always meant business. "I ought to strangle you right here and now. I have never been so goddamned embarrassed in all my life. There's only one thing that keeps me from murdering you, one reason you deserve to stay alive. You've got balls. I've got to give you that." He was shaking his head. "You've got real balls."

The smile on my mother's face never faded. "I guess that means I'll get a present next year."

"Don't push your luck," he said over his shoulder as he turned up the volume on the television.

She had balls all right.

Two things came clear to me at that moment. First of all, with balls you could get away with almost anything. And secondly, whatever it took, whatever I had to do, I was going to get me a set.

Chapter 3

One *Malocchio*, Two *Malocchio*, Three *Malocchio* . . .

THERE WAS one thing even the biggest set of *coglioni* in the universe couldn't protect you from, the *malocchio*—the evil eye.

It is frighteningly simple to put the *malocchio* on someone. You point your index and pinky fingers, holding down the two middle fingers with the thumb. Then you shoot off all your ill will, saying *malocchio, malocchio, malocchio*. And your victim will be duly cursed.

From the moment I achieved the manual dexterity to make the gesture, I was made to understand that this was not a game. Pointing those *malocchio* fingers at another human being was tantamount to aiming a loaded weapon. Make that gesture in an Italian restaurant and you'll see grown men dive for cover.

Of course, not everyone can deliver the *malocchio* with deadly accuracy. The strength of the *malocchio* is proportionately related to the strength of its user and the justifiability of his grievance toward you. For instance, a pissed-off kid, who is presumably not the spawn of Satan, might be able to make you trip and fall, or cause you other minor embarrassment. A wronged business associate could cause a financial setback. A woman scorned could make your dick fall off; or so I'd heard.

But this was all just amateur stuff and nothing compared to what could happen to your life if the *malocchio* were to be put on you by a genuine *strega*, a witch.

If you were lucky, she'd just kill you. But they almost never did that. Not enough pain and suffering involved. No, it was so much better to watch you struggle through life, your heart's desires always just out of your reach.

Okay, so this is what most people call living. But not my father.

My father was convinced that the *malocchio* was real. He was convinced that he was a victim of it. And he had proof.

His paternal grandfather and grandmother only had sons. His father and mother only had sons. His brothers and their wives only had sons. And he and my mother only had daughters. Three of us to be exact. And we all know that bad things happen in threes.

I had the distinction of being the first girl born into my father's family in seventy-five years. That made me special. It made me an aberration. How nice it was to know that not only was I destined to get "the curse," but I actually was the curse.

I never took it too personally though. After all, I was only one of a myriad of "slings and arrows of outrageous fortune" that my father was forced to bear. Everything from a death in the family to a bad hair day (a real catastrophe to a man who stopped in front of every mirror and pulled the comb from his back pocket to tend to his perfect Dean Martin hairdo) was blamed on the *malocchio*.

Oh, how my little heart broke for my father every time he didn't get exactly what he wanted precisely when he wanted it. All because of the *malocchio!*

And here's the best part; the *malocchio* that followed him through life like a perpetual black cloud over his head didn't really belong to him at all. It was a family legacy.

The story goes like this. My grandfather came to this country at the turn of the century when he was in his early twenties and made his fortune as a wine merchant in New York. He married and had a son, my father's older brother. But my grandfather's wife died. And after years of grieving, he finally fell in love again at the age of thirty-five. Unfortunately, the person with whom he fell in love was a girl of fifteen. While this was not so unusual in the Roaring Twenties, her family disapproved of the match. So my fifteen-year-old grandmother ran away from home to marry the man of her dreams.

While her brothers only threatened my grandfather's life, it was the eldest sister who actually took matters into her hands.

It turns out that Aunt Brigit was a genuine *strega*. According to my father (because I never actually met anyone from my grandmother's side of the family), Aunt Brigit had a mustache and a goiter, and I think was hunchbacked. She always wore a black dress with her stockings rolled down below her knees. And she smelled of garlic. Didn't we all? Needless to say, she was the spinster aunt—a *zitella*—and therefore bitter for lots of reasons anyway. So when her fifteen-year-old sister ran off with an older man, who also happened to be quite handsome and rich, it was no surprise to anyone that she put the *malocchio* on the both of them as well as all progeny that might result from their accursed union.

Almost immediately after the marriage, my grandfather lost all his money.

I'd heard stories of just how poor they were when my father was a child. Probably the saddest and most illustrative of these had to do with Christmas.

To make ends meet, my grandmother worked at a five-and-dime store. My grandfather worked at a restaurant. And as Christmas Eve was the busiest night of the year, neither one of them could ever be home with their children.

My grandfather didn't get out of the restaurant until after midnight. But by then, all of the vendors had abandoned what was left of their stock of Christmas trees, so my grandfather could pick through the remainders and bring a tree home to his family without having to dip into the rent or grocery money.

My grandmother brought home whatever decorations she could scavenge from the store displays. And these two exhausted people would spend the night decorating to make the best Christmas they could for their sons.

Presents were scarce. There were none for my grandparents except for the handmade tokens from their children. And in their leanest, meanest year, my father and Uncle Gene had to share a bow-and-arrow set that my grandmother managed to pilfer from the five-and-dime.

While I always knew that my father had a near-fatal predilection for hyperbole, I also knew that the Christmas stories were true. I knew because he took no pleasure in the telling. They were less stories really than they were wounds that would not heal.

And somehow, in his psyche, my father equated that poverty and that pain with being Italian. But because he would never dare verbalize such a thing, not even to himself, he had to find a more palatable explanation.

The *malocchio*.

My father never saw a correlation between Prohibition, the Depression, and the downturn of my grandfather's fortunes. All he knew was that while his older brother had grown up privileged, he and his younger brother had grown up poor. Even his own financial success in life did nothing to dispossess him of his belief in the curse.

I myself began to believe in the *malocchio* when I was five years old and my first sister was born. I very much resented being divested of my "only child" status, so much so that I refused to refer to my sister by name, choosing instead to call her It. I begged my parents constantly to take "It" back where they got It. But It didn't leave.

In fact, two years later, they brought home another one, the Baby. And again I was forced to wonder about the *malocchio*.

My mother insisted that it was all nonsense. But then she could afford to take that attitude. She was a Cascone by marriage, not by birth, and therefore not personally cursed.

As far as my father was concerned, Aunt Brigit was to blame for any and all hardships that befell the family.

I wavered on the subject. I wasn't quite sure how an Aunt "Brigit" got into an Italian family in the first place. And secondly, I refused to accept that I was even marginally related to some bitter old troll with a goiter and a mustache who was hunchbacked.

But whether Aunt Brigit was a real person or just a figment of my father's sublimely overactive imagination, she was an integral part of our family history. Without Aunt Brigit, there was no *malocchio*. And that was simply unthinkable.

There is an upside to being able to claim ownership of a *malocchio*. Any bad thing that happens to you cannot be viewed as your own fault. Whereas any accomplishment is clearly the result of exemplary effort in the face of the insurmountable powers of evil working against you. No matter that the threat of disaster lurked just around every corner. With it came the potential for high drama that we Italians prize above all else.

Chapter 4

≈

Che Disastro!

DESPITE THE fact that my father was sure that he was "snakebitten," his law practice flourished. The wad of cash he carried in his pocket became so substantial that even Mae West couldn't have mistaken it for anything else. And there was enough money in the bank for him to finally buy into the American Dream.

One Sunday afternoon, when I was about nine, he piled us all into the car, refusing to tell us where we were going. But he promised it would be the best surprise in the world.

We drove out of the city, out to a place where there were no kids playing in the streets, then farther still, to a place where there were no streets. I couldn't imagine what kinds of surprises lurked out there. Grizzly bears?

"Where are we going?" my mother asked suspiciously as my father turned the car onto a dirt road that led into some pretty dense woods.

"You'll see," he answered with a sly smile.

I was beginning to worry that he was planning to ditch us all out there like in some grim fairy tale. Little did I know.

He stopped the car and said, "Okay, everybody out." And he said it a little too enthusiastically to my way of thinking.

"What is this all about?" my mother demanded.

Good, I thought. She wasn't going to let us go without a fight.

"See that marker?" My father pointed to a stick in the ground that had an orange ribbon tied around the top of it. He didn't wait for an answer. "That's the beginning of our property line. I just bought this lot. And I'm going to build you a big, brand-new house right up there on top of that hill."

My mother burst into tears.

"What's the matter?" my father asked.

He could be so dense sometimes. What was the matter? We were not a pioneer family. I, for one, was not about to pull up stakes and leave civilized society to go live out in the woods like Daniel Boone, wearing a coonskin cap and forced to eat possum or maybe each other. No, sir.

"I can't believe this," my mother cried. That made two of us. I was pretty confident that my mother was going to put the kibosh on this loony idea. Until she said, "This is the most wonderful thing you've ever done!" She threw her arms around and kissed him.

That was when I started crying.

"Aw, Chicken," my father said as he let go of my mother and headed toward me. "Are you happy too?"

"No," I told him. "No, I am not. I don't want to live out here in the woods."

My father chuckled. "We won't be living in the woods," he said reassuringly. "They're going to build a whole neighborhood here, a neighborhood of big, beautiful houses, all of them with nice big backyards. And ours is going to be the first one."

"So we will be out here all alone." I continued crying.

"Only for a little while," he said.

"That's kind of scary," my middle sister, It, piped up, obviously unnerved by my reaction.

I was relieved to know that I was getting through to someone. "Kind of scary?" I said to her. "It's real scary. We don't know anything about living in the woods. Who knows what could happen to us out here. We'll never be able to go out after dark. And even in the daytime we'll have to bring bread crumbs with us every time we leave the house just so we can find our way back."

"I don't want to live here either," It announced, convinced by my argument.

"Me neither," the Baby chimed in, not because she understood what was going on, but because she always had to follow her two older sisters.

"Three against two," I told my father.

"Do something," my mother said to him. That meant I was his responsibility.

"Let's take a walk," he said. That never meant anything but trouble. "Let's take a walk" or "Let's go for a ride in the car" were nothing more than euphemisms for "You will be held hostage until you comply with all my demands." No wonder he was so good in the courtroom; he was playing to a captive audience there too.

Before I could protest, he had his arm around me and was propelling me forward, up the hill to the site of our new homestead. "Baby, don't you see how wonderful this is going to be?"

Leaving my home? Leaving my friends? "No."

"See where we're standing right now? In just a few months, there's going to be a great big house right here. Our house. And it's going to have a great big living room. And a great big dining room. And a great big kitchen. And a great big family room with a great big TV."

Okay, that was interesting.

He noticed the glimmer in my eye and went on. "And you'll have your own bedroom, twice as big as the one you have to share with your sister now."

This was starting to sound pretty good.

"Both your sisters will have their own rooms too. And there will be an extra bedroom for company so you can invite your friends to come and stay overnight."

But then, my father was known to exaggerate. "Really?"

"Of course. And guess what else."

"What?" I asked cautiously. I didn't want to get swept away and agree to anything prematurely.

"We're going to have a built-in pool in the backyard too. Now what do you think?"

"I don't know," I answered honestly. It sure sounded like a lot of great stuff. But it was a lot of great stuff out in the middle of nowhere.

"It'll be a whole new life for us," my father enthused.

"But I like our old life," I said simply.

"Hmm," my father grunted thoughtfully, clearly perplexed. After a minute he said, "I guess I never really gave enough thought to how this would make you feel. I think about where we live now and all I see is a crummy little house that's too small for my family. But for you, it's home—the only home you've ever known. And you feel safe there."

"And happy," I added. In my little neighborhood, I belonged. I knew everybody. And they knew me. I knew all the rules there.

I knew how to work them. And I knew how to break them sometimes too. I knew when to stand up and fight for myself, and when to walk away. And at the end of the day, I went to sleep secure in the knowledge that tomorrow would be the same game with the same rules and the same players. Wasn't that the way life was supposed to be?

He nodded his understanding. For a moment, I thought we were going to walk away from this place, get in the car and go home, and forget all about it. But my hopes were quickly dashed. "Let me explain something to you, Baby," my father started.

In my experience, whenever somebody had to explain something to you, it usually meant they wanted you to do something that you knew in your heart and in your guts was not going to be right for you. Since my father was an expert at explaining things to people, I realized at that moment that all hope was lost. Before I knew what hit me, I'd be living in this godforsaken place.

"You can't spend your whole life in just one place," he went on.

That was news to me, since most of the people I knew did just that. "Why not?" I asked him. "If you're happy, why can't you stay where you are?"

He didn't bother to say that he and my mother weren't really happy where we were. He didn't have to. I'd already gathered that. "It's a great big world out there, Baby."

A great big world. A great big house. A great big television. I saw that there was a theme developing. I just didn't understand it. And I was pretty sure I wasn't going to like it.

"A great big world," he repeated. "Full of things that you haven't even begun to imagine. There's so much to see and so much to do. And none of it's on Melrose Avenue."

"Well, if you ask me, it doesn't look like it's here either."

He laughed. It was his gentle laugh, his understanding laugh, his "I'm not laughing at you" laugh. "I can see your point," he said, still laughing. Then he changed direction abruptly. "Do you remember Grandpop?"

It was a stupid question, so stupid I didn't bother to answer it. My face told him all he needed to know. Tears welled up in my eyes at the very mention of his name. Did I remember my grandfather? How could I forget him? I loved him more than anyone in the whole world, more than my parents, more than anybody else that would ever come into my life.

For the first four years of my life, he was my constant companion. He and my grandmother lived with us in our little semi-detached, rented house. My father was in law school. My mother worked to support the family. My grandmother took care of all the domestic chores. And my grandfather got me.

And I got everything I ever asked for and more.

My grandparents and I had our own private language. It was a beautiful language, a language of love. My mother didn't know how to speak it. And my father wasn't allowed to, at least not in front of my grandfather. Whenever my father would try, my grandfather would shake his head in dismay and say, *"Parli italiano come una vacca spagnola."* It meant, "You speak Italian like a Spanish cow."

It was funny to me to hear my father stumble over words in our language when he clearly had such great command of his own. But as far as I could tell, that was the only thing he had command of in our house. He certainly had no control over me. As long as my grandfather was in earshot, nobody ever reprimanded me or told me no. Needless to say, I never strayed very far from my grandfather's side. He was the first person I wanted to see every morning, and he was the one to tell me my bedtime story at night.

I was so attached to my grandfather that I couldn't bear to let him leave the house without me. One day while my grandmother was out food shopping and my mother was at work, my grandfather said that he too had to go out for a while. It shouldn't have been a big deal because my father didn't have classes that day and so he was at home to look after me.

I was thrilled to have Daddy home to play with me. He was a wonderful playmate. There was no one in the world more eager to learn the tricks and gambols of childhood than he was. But I always felt that he really needed the supervision of an adult, even more than I did.

So when Grandpop headed for the door to leave that afternoon, I panicked. I ran to the door and grabbed on to the edge of it to pull it open even as he was closing it from the other side. My little fingers got smashed hard between the door and the frame.

The moment he heard me howl and realized what had happened, my grandfather came rushing back inside to comfort me.

While my father nearly fainted when he saw that the nail on my index finger was purple from the amount of blood that had pooled up beneath it, my grandfather picked me up and rocked me and assured us both that it would be okay.

And it was, because he never did leave the house that day.

But then suddenly, one morning not long after, he was gone for good. I wasn't allowed to go into his bedroom to wake him up the way I always did. My father kept me out. He told me that Grandpop wasn't there anymore, that he had gone to heaven during the night. He told me that Grandpop didn't want to leave me but that he had to go, that he was someplace better and that he'd always be watching over me even though I couldn't see him. My father tried to make it all sound okay, but I knew it wasn't okay because he couldn't stop crying. My mother cried too. So did my uncle and my aunt and my grandmother and everybody else who came to our house that day. But everybody assured me that it was okay.

Two weeks later they were still insisting that everything was going to be okay when my other grandfather "went to heaven." And a week after that, they were all sticking to the same story when my grandmom—my father's mother—went to join Grandpop in heaven.

From the whispering that went on among the adults, I learned that each of my grandfathers had died of a heart attack and that my grandmother had died of cancer. I didn't understand anything about heaven or heart attacks or cancer. But one thing I knew beyond a shadow of a doubt was that none of it was okay. In a lot of ways, it would never be okay again.

My mother and father were twenty-four and twenty-five years old. They were devastated by the loss of three parents in just one month's time. It was a memory they worked very hard to banish from their lives. As a result, it was rare to hear either one of them speak about the parents who had died.

So when my father invoked the memory of my grandfather that day up on the hill in the woods that my father wanted me to come to view as "home," I knew that he was trying to tell me something that was very important to him.

"Baby, you understand that Grandpop came to this country from somewhere else," he started.

"Italy," I told him. In the four years since my grandfather had died, I had come to understand that the "secret" language that we spoke was actually a real language somewhere else in the world. It was the place where my grandfather had been born. It was what made him a "ginker."

That was what they called first-generation Italians in our neighborhood. "Ginkers." They were the courtly, old gentlemen who wore jackets and ties and hats even after they'd retired and were spending their days in the park playing bocce ball.

Somehow, their sons became "goombas." *Goomba* is a bastardization of the Italian word *compare*. It means "buddy" or "pal."

Neither one of those monikers was particularly flattering.

"He's just an old ginker" was always said with a shrug and a shake of the head. It meant, "He's just an old man, with Old World values, who hasn't the vaguest notion how to survive here in America, the Promised Land." Whereas "He's a real goomba" usually came with a wink and the connotation that the person in question was open to any kind of illegal activity.

My father had spent his entire life running away from both of those words.

But I was too young to understand epithets. All I knew was that somehow I belonged to the place of my grandfather's origin. "Grandpop came from Italy," I said proudly. "I want to go there."

"Someday," my father said. He smiled and he stroked my face. He was looking at me, but I could tell that he was seeing something far, far away too. "Anyway," he said, shaking himself out of it, "Grandpop came to this country to find a better life. He came looking for the American Dream."

I saw the lure. "And what's that?" I bit.

"It's this," my father answered, spreading his arms, gesturing to show that he meant our surroundings.

"The woods?" I grimaced. I knew my grandfather. He was no Daniel Boone. My grandfather grew up on the Bay of Naples in a small town called Castellammare di Stabia. He told me that when he was a little boy, he would sit on the cliffs and watch the fishing boats in the bay. He told me that it was the most beautiful place in the world. "Grandpop did not come here to live in the woods," I said with authority.

"How many times do I have to tell you, it's not going to be woods. We're going to live in a big house, the kind of house that Grandpop wanted for his family, the kind of house he would be proud of."

So there it was. Right before my eyes, my father had become a child again. While this was not really an unusual occurrence—not the childish behavior anyway—I found myself lost in empathy with the part of him that wanted to please his father. It was all I ever wanted to do too.

"Okay, Daddy, if this is where you want to live, then this is where we'll live." I told him what he wanted to hear. As if it were my decision to make. I understood full well that the family did not spin around my whims, not anymore, not since my grandfather had died.

"I only wish Grandpop could have lived to see this," my father said. The words caught in his throat and his eyes welled up with tears. "I wish I could have brought him here to live." He was lost in his daydreams. "Yeah," he said more to himself than to me. "My old man would have loved this place." He looked at me as if for confirmation. My face must not have provided it. "So will you," he said.

Somehow, I doubted it.

⤨

Immigration and Denaturalization

IT DIDN'T take long for word to spread in our little neigh-borhood that we were moving out. It seemed to become a great cause of celebration to everyone who heard the news. It wasn't that they were happy to see us go. "We'll miss you so much," was always the first thing anybody said about it. But right after that, they'd shake their heads and force a smile and say to my parents, "You did it! You made it out. Good for you. I hope someday we can save up enough money to get out of here too."

All of a sudden, we were special; we'd "made it out." But what did that mean? I tried time and time again to understand that statement. But all my efforts were for naught. It simply made no sense to me. Made it out? It wasn't as if our neighborhood was surrounded by bars. There were no guards or dogs keeping us put. As far as I knew, my parents weren't busy digging tunnels in the night in order to make the great escape. And frankly, I was pretty sure that if all these well-wishers had seen where we were headed, they would have quickly changed their tune.

But everybody seemed to have American Dream fever that summer. In school we were told that our forefathers had defined that as "life, liberty, and the pursuit of happiness." On television, Superman defended "truth, justice, and the American way." But what I was quickly learning was that what it really meant was a bigger house, a bigger car, and more money. And as far as I could tell, all that added up to was just isolation.

"Your friends are just jealous," my parents would tell me whenever I'd complain that I'd been left out of yet another trip to the movies, or the pizza parlor, or the five-and-dime, or just an afternoon of swimming in someone's "dinky-above-ground pool."

But the other kids in the neighborhood didn't really seem jealous to me. They didn't seem to want to be going where I was going. They weren't even all that interested in where I was going. All that really mattered to them was that I was going. That made them unhappy. It made them angry. It made them treat me as something of a traitor. While I never got the feeling that I was being purposefully ostracized, I did begin to feel that I had become as invisible as a ghost much of the time. It was as if my friends were practicing how they would behave when I wasn't there anymore.

The old neighborhood was lost to me. The new neighborhood wasn't even built yet. Here was the problem: I still existed. But somehow, I just wasn't there anymore. I wasn't anywhere.

That was the summer I learned to travel without moving an inch. I spent nearly all of my time locked up in my room with my nose in a book. I visited different places, different times, and different worlds. Any story that involved knights in shining armor was sure to captivate my imagination—though I, of course, never pictured myself as the damsel in distress but rather as the one wielding the sword.

Since reading was such a noble activity, nobody ever bothered me. And I never bothered anybody else. I quietly learned to adapt to being invisible.

I was quite certain that by the time I left the only home I had ever known, nobody would even notice that I had gone. And when we moved into our new home, there would be nobody there to notice that I had arrived. The American Dream was proving to be a nightmare to me. Still, my parents were happy.

Every weekend we would all pile into the car and drive out to nowhere-ville to inspect the progress of the dream house. I can't say that I found it entirely uninteresting. In fact, I found it fascinating that a hole in the ground could become a concrete basement, that skeletal wooden beams became walls, that a staircase to nowhere suddenly provided access to a vast second floor. Bare pipes came to support sinks, bathtubs, toilets, and shower stalls. Windows and doors filled in gaping holes in the walls. Flagstone and tile and polished wood and plush carpet appeared underfoot. And the once muddy lot was transformed into parklike perfection with a layer of emerald green sod.

When it was finished, it was like nothing I had ever seen before, except maybe in the movies. And to me, it seemed every bit as ethereal.

The furniture arrived the weekend before we did. I sat on the front porch with my sisters, on the new wrought iron decorative outdoor furniture, and watched my mother direct a crew of Teamsters as they transformed our faux colonial house into an Ethan Allen showroom.

Aside from our clothes and personal belongings, nothing was coming with us from the old house except a few "good" things—china, silver, crystal, art, and memorabilia. Everything else was being given away to family, friends, or the Salvation Army.

When the furniture van finally left, emptied of its contents, my sisters and I followed our parents on an inspection tour of our new abode. While my parents were intoxicated by the new-life smell of the place, I felt disoriented, lost, and frighteningly alone. The view from nearly every window was empty lots, mountains of dirt, construction equipment, and houses in various stages of development. There were no people.

My own bedroom was tucked into a back corner of the house. It was clearly a position of privilege, befitting the firstborn, in absence of the much-desired son. The only other room with more privacy and a better view was the master bedroom.

Still, I hated it. I hated the royal blue carpet and powder blue walls, despite the fact that I had chosen the colors myself. I hated the canopied bed and the froufrou linens that adorned it even though I'd okayed them in the store. I hated the dresser and mirror and the vanity table and chair. And I especially hated the reproduction painting of *The Girl with Watering Can*. I hated her long, blond curls and Victorian dress, and high-buttoned shoes, and her lonely, haunted expression staring out at me from inside the heavy, gilt frame.

But when my parents said to me, "What do you think?" I couldn't bring myself to tell them the truth. "It's nice," I said, using the old standard. "It's really nice. I like it a lot." I was hoping that they would pick up on the zombielike tone of my voice, that they would call me on the lie. But they didn't. They couldn't. They had too much invested.

"Our new home," my father announced proudly. "We move in the day after tomorrow. And we'll never look back."

That was the American Dream. It's called a dream because it is delusional. It is something that can never hold up under the harsh light of day.

Chapter 6

These Hands Were Made
for Talkin'

THERE IS an old joke that if you want to get an Italian to
shut up, make him sit on his hands. In our family, that
was no joke. It was a simple fact of life and, sometimes, an
amusing parlor game. We actually had competitions called "Sit
on your hands and tell me a story." The point was to see who
could speak for the longest amount of time without moving his
hands.

My father always lost. Always.

The man simply couldn't keep his hands still. Or his mouth
shut.

Good thing for us he made his living by talking. I never had to wonder why a lawyer was sometimes referred to as a "mouth-piece." And nobody had to tell me that my father was the best of the best.

My mother kept scrapbooks of newspaper clippings that documented one courtroom victory after another. But she never let it go to his head.

"My summation was brilliant," he crowed one night at dinner, regaling us with the story of how he'd won yet another grueling case.

"You talked for six straight hours," my mother pointed out, unimpressed.

"Yes," he said, undaunted. "And I did it all without notes."

"Do you want to know why you really won?" My mother didn't wait for an answer. To be perfectly honest, my mother could, as my father often pointed out, "talk the balls off a brass monkey." "You won because when they locked up the jury, the foreman said, 'Look, if we don't give that guy what he wants, they may let him come back and talk to us again.' "

"Ha, ha," my father groaned.

The rest of us laughed in earnest. We knew it was probably true.

That man loved to hear the sound of his own voice. Apparently, he always had. He told me once that his earliest memory was at about two years old. He was sitting on the floor in the kitchen, playing with a toy while his mother cooked dinner. His father came into the kitchen, looked down at him, and shook his head. "What's wrong with that kid?" he said to my grandmother. "He's always talking to himself."

It never stopped. Even if he wasn't making any sound, I could tell when he was talking to himself just by watching his hands move.

But as often as his mouth got him—and others—out of trouble, his hands got him into it.

One Saturday afternoon, when we'd been in the house for almost a year and I had begun to realize that I was fighting a losing battle against suburban ennui, my sisters and I were playing contentedly on the front lawn. It was one of those rare occasions when my mother actually left us alone while she went to the grocery store. We shouldn't have had to be alone because my father ought to have been there to take care of us. But he had to go to his office to pick up some papers, and he was taking an awfully long time getting back.

Before my mother left, she made a big deal about how much she trusted me to be in charge and how she just knew that my sisters would behave and nothing would go wrong. That was, of course, after she made an even bigger deal about how intolerably irresponsible my father was and how she couldn't trust him as far as she could spit. I knew it was all bullshit—well, except the part about my father. I knew she didn't so much trust us, as she needed to get away from us for a little while.

It had been a rough morning for her. First, I had dropped my Shake-a-Puddin'—which I wasn't supposed to be having for breakfast anyway—on the kitchen floor when my mother had startled me by catching me in the act. When the cup hit the floor, it exploded like a pudding bomb. We even had to get the ladder to clean pudding off the ceiling—chocolate, of course.

She'd no sooner finished yelling at me than she discovered that my middle sister had put her box of Crayola 64s into the dryer to hide them from our baby sister. The "Egyptian cotton" bath towels came out with a whole new look. They looked like Walt Disney had puked all over them. My mother started yelling again. But we never heard a word. We just stood there watching in abject terror as she turned all sixty-four colors.

In an attempt to calm herself, she decided to take a bath. That was when my baby sister decided to deliver the coup de grace. She toddled into the bathroom and poured the box of

Rice Krispies she was carrying right into the bathtub with my mother. It's amazing how sticky Rice Krispies become in water. My mother was so covered with them that she didn't need clothes to be considered "decent." It took her the rest of the morning to get them all off. She said she was picking Rice Krispies out of places she didn't know she had.

Meanwhile, my father slept soundly.

All in all, it was pretty much just a regular Saturday morning in our house. The thing that had my mother so tense was that she was throwing a dinner party that evening.

She needed to get a few things from the food store and she didn't have time to be giving out beatings in the cupcake and candy aisles. Hence, her newfound trust in our ability to take care of ourselves.

My sisters and I actually had the sneaking suspicion that she was hoping we'd all run away from home while she was gone. And that's exactly why we were behaving like perfect little angels. That, and the fact that she'd promised to bring home enough goodies to put us all into a sugar coma.

So there we were, sitting on the front lawn, enjoying a friendly game of Mouse Trap when a bright red sports car flashed by and sped up our driveway.

Being the one in charge, I sprang to my feet to investigate. At first I was nervous, frightened even. Strange cars were never to be trusted, even cool, little red ones. But just as I was about to instruct my sisters to go inside the house, I noticed that while the car was strange, the driver was strangely familiar.

"Daddy!" I began running toward the driveway, my sisters right on my heels.

"Stay back," my father hollered out the window.

We obeyed. Not because we were obedient, but because we were startled and confused.

"Is something wrong?" I asked suspiciously.

He ignored my question and asked one of his own. "Where's your mother?"

"At the food store," I told him.

"Good." He was definitely trying to get away with something. "Do we have any olive oil in the house?"

As usual, the conversation with my father had gotten completely away from me. "Huh?"

"It's a simple question, Baby." He glared at me as though I were the one who was nuts. "Do we have any olive oil in the house?"

Instead of troubling myself with the obvious question of why a man in a red sports car wanted olive oil, I focused solely on the practical aspects of his inquiry. "That is a stupid question."

There were things we ran out of. Regularly. Milk. Bread. Butter. Eggs. My favorite cereal. Ice cream. But olive oil? Never. It was like asking if we had any air in the house.

"Of course we have olive oil," I told him. "Why?"

"Never mind, wise guy. Just listen to me and do what I say. Stay away from the car!" he barked at my baby sister who was trying to sneak up on him. "You." He pointed to me. "Go in the house and fill a cup with olive oil and bring it out here to me."

"Mommy is going to be mad, isn't she?" my middle sister snickered. Seeing him get into trouble was much more fun for us kids than seeing it happen to one another.

"No. Mommy is not going to be mad," he lied. "In the first place, there is nothing for Mommy to be mad about. And secondly, she is never even going to know that I was here."

Our faces said otherwise.

"Do you know why she is never going to know? Because there's twenty bucks in it for everybody who forgets to tell her about this."

Twenty bucks! Each! He was in it deep. But my mother was

due home any minute, and if I was going to pocket twenty bucks, there was no time to be asking questions. I dashed into the house, grabbed one of my mother's Lenox teacups, and filled it with 100 percent pure, virgin, cold-pressed olive oil.

My twenty bucks were in the bag. But while I should have been imagining all the wonderful things I could do with that much money, I suddenly became curious about why my father needed a cup of olive oil in a beautiful red sports car.

To try and get to the bottom of that mystery, I did something I rarely allowed myself to do. "Think like him," I instructed myself. This was a risky business, rather like making funny faces. "What if you were to get stuck like that forever?" my mother would threaten whenever she caught me making faces at someone. While being stuck forever with your eyelids turned inside out and a pig nose was a pretty scary thought, it paled in comparison to the thought of being stuck forever in my father's psyche. It was a fun place to visit, but I didn't want to live there.

"Where have you been?" my father griped as I moved toward the car haltingly.

That was when it hit me. I knew exactly what he intended to do with the olive oil. "Uh-uh." I shook my head as I stepped backward.

"Baby, I've got no time to fool around," my father growled. "Give me that olive oil. Now!"

There was nothing for me to do but try to explain to him the error in his thinking. This seldom worked. But none of us ever stopped trying. "Listen to me, Daddy." I spoke slowly and calmly, the way I'd seen cops do it in movies when they were trying to talk somebody off a ledge. "When the oil light goes on in the car, I'm pretty sure it does not mean that the car wants olive oil." I was also pretty sure I had just figured out why his cars were always breaking down. "You have to take the car to the gas station and they put a different kind of oil in it. It's black and gooey. But it's definitely what you're supposed to put in a car. I know this because a couple of weeks ago, I was in the car with Mommy and that's what we did when her oil light went on."

"Baby, what do you think I am, stupid?"

That was not a rhetorical question. I simply chose not to answer it.

"I am not going to put the olive oil into the car," he assured me. "I need it for something else. Now give me the cup," my father repeated. "Then all of you go inside."

I don't know why I did it, but I gave him the cup. None of us moved.

"Get out of here." He jerked his head in the direction of the house.

"Not without our twenty bucks," my middle sister said, reminding him of our deal.

"I'll give it to you later," he promised.

"Uh-uh," we said in unison.

"Mommy will be home any minute," I reminded him. "And I'll bet she's going to have a lot of questions about where you've been all day and what you're doing with this fancy red car."

With the right tactics, it is possible to elicit a full confession from anybody. In our house, the thought of having to face the wrath of my mother was just about all the strong-arming that was ever required. My father's tough-guy veneer crumbled under that pressure.

"Okay," he surrendered. "It went like this. I was on my way home from the office when I noticed a brand-new Jaguar dealership. So I pulled in just to have a look. I got to talking to one of the salesmen and he offered to let me take this car for a test drive. What was I supposed to do, say no?"

"So are we keeping it?" I was suddenly excited by the prospect.

"We may have to," he groaned.

"Did you already break it?" I braced myself for the bad news.

"No," he said. But it wasn't reassuring. It was the kind of "no" that really meant "if only it were just that." "I'm stuck in it."

"Stuck?" That made no sense at all to me. "How are you stuck?"

"My finger," he admitted.

We all moved in for a look.

"It's not as stupid as it looks," he said defensively. "I was stopped at a red light and I was getting bored. So I started doing this." He demonstrated with his free hand.

The steering wheel of the Jaguar was connected to its hub by three flat metal bars. Each bar had three holes of graduated size. The largest hole was closest to the hub, and the smallest was closest to the steering wheel. Apparently, as he was sitting at the stoplight, he was poking his index fingers into the holes, moving from the hub to the steering wheel and back again. And again. And again. Until . . .

"That's how my finger got stuck."

It was stuck all right. Stuck in the smallest hole. Stuck, and swollen, and turning a little purple.

"Can I please have the olive oil now?"

It took some work. But we finally got him free, thus reaffirming his belief in the magical powers of olive oil.

"How long were you driving around like that?" I asked him.

"A long time. And it wasn't easy, especially turning corners. I don't want to talk about it anymore. Besides, I've got to fill this car up with gas and get it back before they think I've stolen it."

My sisters held out their palms and wriggled their fingers in reminder.

"Oh, yeah." He reached into his pocket, peeled off three

twenties, and handed them over. Then he looked at his poor, mangled finger and drove off without saying another word.

With his finger as badly injured as it was, I figured he'd be mute for at least a week. Or maybe that was just wishful thinking.

But he was absolutely certain that all the money he'd passed out had bought our silence for a lifetime. Now that was wishful thinking!

Chapter 7

≈

Time to Kill
the Dinner

MY FATHER ought to have learned that there are some places where one's fingers simply do not belong. He was a brilliant man, but somehow life's little lessons always managed to elude him. He didn't have much luck with the big ones either.

Not long after he'd gotten his finger stuck in the steering wheel of a Jaguar, he had another, more painful mishap.

Once again, it was a Saturday. Saturday always seemed to be "anything-can-happen day" in our house. That was because we were all at home, without structured activities, and my father had a take-charge attitude.

On this particular Saturday, my father decided that what he

was going to take charge of that day was dinner. Not the food gathering or preparation, mind you. That was my mother's job. It was taxing enough for him to wrestle with the decision of what it was he really wanted.

Most juries spent less time deliberating the fate of his clients than he spent contemplating his dinner. He approached every meal as though it might be his last. Which may not have been all that far-fetched really, since my mother was always threatening.

After spending the entire morning carefully weighing all the options, my father finally settled on what was probably the most labor-intensive dish in my mother's repertoire. It was also, inarguably, one of the best. His final verdict was that we would be having spaghetti and crabs for dinner. My sisters and I cheered. My mother groaned and got in the car to go to the fish market to buy three dozen crabs—a dozen for my father and a half-dozen each for the rest of us.

She did not have to stop at the food store to pick up the other ingredients: chopped tomatoes, tomato paste, tomato puree, olive oil, garlic, parsley, oregano, basil, wine, and pasta. These were things she had on hand, and always in large enough quantities to get us through a nuclear winter.

My father was so excited by the thought of his dinner that he had us kids pull out all the things that my mother would need to prepare it. By the time she got home, everything was neatly laid out on the counter and three giant pots of water were at full boil on the stove.

It was time for the killing to begin.

My mother brought the three large, brown paper bags full of live crabs into the kitchen.

Meanwhile, my father was in the family room, lying on the couch, watching a ball game.

I had long since given up complaining that he got to loaf around while I had to help. It wasn't that I was persuaded by his argument that he worked hard all week and deserved to relax on the weekends. It was that my mother made me understand that we were better off when he was quiet and out of the way.

"Ready?" she asked me as she unrolled the top of the first bag.

We both winced. It was a hateful job. Despite the fact that crabs have a cuteness factor of minus ten, they are still God's creatures. And as such, dumping them into a pot of boiling water and slapping the lid on to bar any hope of escape was always a little bit traumatizing both to me and to my mother.

"Let's do it," she said.

I picked up the lid and held it close to the pot as she emptied the contents of the first bag. As soon as the last crab hit the water, I slammed down the lid. We both heaved a sigh of relief. One down, two to go.

We handled the second bag with equal efficiency.

But, unbeknownst to my mother, the third bag had a tear in the side, and as she was emptying the crabs into the pot, three fell from the bag onto the floor.

The screaming began instantaneously. As the crabs skittered along the floor, my mother and I scrambled up onto the countertops.

My sisters, who were upstairs playing, hurried to the kitchen. As soon as they saw the problem, they too began screaming and retreated immediately. "Daddy! Daddy!" they cried in unison, heading for the family room to the person they erroneously associated with safety and protection.

"Jesus Christ Almighty," he grumbled as he came into the kitchen. "What the hell is going on in here?"

"Look out! Look out!" my mother shrieked as he nearly stepped on a crab in his stocking feet.

"Jesus Christ!" he repeated almost in my mother's pitch as he too hopped up onto the counter.

"Now what?" I demanded. "Are we all just going to sit up here until they die of old age or something?"

My father gave me a dirty look and slid off the counter into a crab-free zone. "I don't know what you two yo-yos are so afraid of." Despite the bravado in his voice, I noticed that he was keeping a close eye on the three escaped crabs as well as staying a safe distance away from them.

"All right." He sighed. "Let me take care of this. Do we have any tongs in this kitchen?"

My mother and I both pointed to the drawer where she kept those kinds of tools. It never ceased to amaze me that while my father lived there just like the rest of us, he never seemed to know where anything was. I once heard him ask my mother where she kept the water glasses. And then he didn't actually get one himself but waited for her to do it for him.

This time she wasn't moving. So he was forced to get the tongs. Once he had them in hand, he carefully snuck up on the first crab, snatched him from behind, and tossed him into the still uncovered pot with the rest of his buddies. He captured the second one with equal aplomb and sent him to meet his maker as well. He was just about to do the same with the third when he suddenly turned away from the stove and released the crab into the sink instead.

"What are you doing?" my mother asked as the two of us climbed down off the counter.

"I'm going to teach you a lesson," he announced.

"And exactly what would that be?" It wasn't that my mother was interested in learning any lessons from my father. She'd long since given up any hope that that was possible. It was just that when disaster struck, as it inevitably would, she wanted to be clear on his original intent.

"I'm going to show you that there is no reason in the world

to be afraid of crabs. I mean, honest to God, what's the worst thing they can do to you?"

My mother didn't say anything. She obviously didn't want to play. So it was up to me to answer his question. "Well, for starters, if they grab you with those claws, they can hurt you. A lot."

"Is that so?" His tone of voice said it wasn't. "What do you say we do a little experiment to find out?"

"Don't do it, Daddy," I warned him. "Don't stick your finger in his claw."

"Why does everybody in this house talk to me like I'm stupid?"

Rhetorical question? Maybe. But even if it wasn't, my mother and I were hiding behind the Fifth Amendment on that one.

"I am not going to stick my finger in his claw. I'm going to use something else to show you." It took just a few seconds for him to find the perfect object. He pulled the straw out of the soda I'd been drinking and began taunting the crab with it. "See?" he said smugly as the crab refused to take the bait. He forced the straw into the crab's claw. He jiggled it around. Still, the crab didn't clamp down on it.

"That doesn't prove anything," I said. "Why would he care about the straw anyway? He knows it's not food."

"Okay," my father conceded. "Let's see what he does with food then." He went into the goodies cabinet and got a piece of licorice. The results were the same. "Now are you satisfied? There is absolutely no reason to be afraid of crabs. Or their claws. How much damage did you think they could do with something so small?" To punctuate his point, he poked at the crab's claw with his finger.

The sound that came out of my father next was like nothing I'd ever heard before, except maybe on *Wild Kingdom*. He began flailing his arm around wildly with the whole crab attached to his finger by that one little claw. Apparently, size really doesn't matter, at least not as it applies to pounds per square inch of pressure. My father yowled in pain as he tried frantically to shake off the crab. But it held fast. My father's face was beet red, and tears of agony welled up in his eyes. In one last, desperate attempt to free his finger and end his suffering, he slammed the crab down onto the counter as hard as he could.

It worked. Sort of. Most of the crab went sliding across the counter, but its claw remained behind, still firmly attached to my father's finger.

"Get it off me," he begged my mother.

"Just a minute," she told him as she went after his assailant with the tongs. Good thinking on her part, since the crab was still alive and still had one good claw with which to attack somebody else. She tossed him into the water, thereby ending all threat of danger, and turned her attention to my father.

After some effort—and a few new expletives from my father—she removed the claw and threw that into the pot too. Waste not, want not.

My father's finger was in pretty bad shape. Not only was it red and swollen this time, but the skin was broken as well. It wasn't so bad that he needed stitches, or so my mother determined. But the fact that there was blood involved—his blood to be specific—implied to my father that this was a catastrophe of epic proportions. As my mother applied Mercurochrome and Band-Aids, my father ranted about tetanus and gangrene and even rabies.

Yeah, he'd taught us all a lesson all right. We learned beyond the shadow of a doubt that we were much better off when he was quiet and out of the way.

It took my mother some time to accomplish that. She had to get him pillows, a blanket, an icepack, and a drink—scotch on the rocks—to ease his pain. But once he was back on the couch in front of the television, we were free to make the dinner.

Spaghetti and Crabs

Step 1: Get a bottle of Chianti. Get the biggest wineglass you can find. Fill it with Chianti and start drinking.

Step 2: Kill as many crabs as you think you can eat by steaming them to death. This is not the worst part of the job. That's up next.

Step 3: Break off the hard outer shell of the crab, and scrape out all the green, slimy innards. Soak the disemboweled crabs in cold water until ready to use. Note: By the time you finish this process, all your fingernails will be broken and your hands will feel as though you've run them through a paper shredder. But it will be well worth it in the end.

Step 4: Prepare the sauce. For each dozen crabs, you will need one pot of sauce. Note: It is called sauce. Only a *cafone* would call it gravy. Of course a *cafone,* a *maleducato* (loosely translated, a lowlife) also pronounces the word *cafone* as *gavone.*

Sauce for Crabs, Shrimp, and Other Seafood

Step 1: Pour the best-quality pure virgin, cold-pressed, first-press (if you can get it) olive oil into a pot big enough to hold a dozen large crabs in SAUCE. How much olive oil? Enough to just cover the bottom of the pot. How many tablespoons is that? I don't know. In my world, measuring devices were used only in baking. And even then, it was only discretionary.

Step 2: Put the pot with the olive oil on a low flame. I have no idea what to tell you to do if you have an electric stove. We always cook with gas. And we always—always—cook with a low flame.

Step 3: Stir fresh, chopped garlic into the oil for flavor. How much garlic? As much as you like. I like at least half a bulb.

Step 4: Time for the tomatoes. Note: A purist would use fresh, preferably homegrown tomatoes. For years, my mother conned my father into believing that was exactly what she was doing. She lied. She was using cans just like everybody else. So here's the measurement in cans. One thirty-two-ounce can of chopped tomatoes. Two thirty-two-ounce cans of tomato puree. And one eight-ounce can of tomato paste whisked smooth in about three cups of water. Pour into the pot with olive oil and garlic. Keep on low flame.

Step 5: Add chopped parsley, chopped oregano, and chopped basil to the pot. Note: It is best to use fresh herbs. But dried herbs will do. How much of each? Again, I don't know. Start with a tablespoon or two and adjust to suit your own taste. Same goes for the salt and pepper you should add at this point. If you like your sauce a little spicy (*al diavolo*), add a little crushed pepper.

Step 6: Take that bottle of Chianti you've been drinking and pour some into the pot. Start with about a cupful and add more as you see fit.

Step 7: Stir sauce and let simmer, loosely covered (with the lid of the pot tipped the slightest bit to allow steam to escape), for about half an hour. Taste. Adjust ingredients if necessary.

Step 8: Add crabs (a dozen or so per pot of sauce) and simmer for another two or three hours. Stir and taste frequently.

This is the real secret to Italian cooking. It is not a science; it is an art, a feast for the senses—all of them. Yes, even hearing. Because after enough practice, you can tell by the sounds coming from your pot if the flame is too high, if something is burning (even before you smell it), or if it's just bubbling away perfectly.

From start to finish, every meal is a drama, some more memorable than others.

For my father, this was one he never would forget—though he never held himself accountable for the injuries he sustained.

When the dinner was brought to the table, my father went searching for the crab with one claw with the same ferocity and sense of divine retribution that possessed Captain Ahab in his quest for the white whale. Fortunately, the crab was already dead. So our story had no tragic ending.

We enjoyed our spaghetti and crabs as heartily as we ever had. But my father took special pleasure in eating the crab with one claw. He even commented on how it tasted so much better than all the others. He made it sound so good, that on some visceral level, I felt cheated. And yet I knew that if I had taken a bite, it would have tasted no different to me from all the rest.

What my father found so delicious was not the crabmeat itself, but the sweet taste of vendetta.

Chapter 8

≈

Eels in the Bathtub

WEEKEND MEALS may have been a production, but they were nothing compared to the helter-skelter that preceded a holiday feast.

And of all the traditions my grandfather brought with him to this country, none was more sacred to us than Christmas Eve dinner.

It was the night we anticipated all year long. A night of great celebration, when family and friends gathered together in peace and joy and—most importantly—serious gluttony.

Because we were Napoletani—people from the Bay of Naples—the Christmas feast was a seafood extravaganza. Anything with gills or shells was sure to show up on our table in one form or another. We fried it, marinated it, baked it, broiled it, sautéed it, or plunked it into sauce. And from about six in the evening until well after midnight we ate, and we ate, and we ate, until every delicious morsel was gone.

There was only one rule on Christmas Eve. No one left the table without eating eel.

We ate eel on Christmas Eve to bring us good luck in the coming year. Since everything we ever did seemed to be motivated by the belief that it would either bring good luck or help us avoid bad luck, no one in the family ever questioned this practice. But newcomers always needed a little bit of coaxing, especially after they were told how the dish was prepared.

Christmas Eels

Step 1: Buy live eels. These are black sea snakes, about two to three feet long. You won't find them in your local grocery store. They can only be found in port cities with large ethnic populations. We got ours from Philadelphia.

Step 2: Bring them home and keep them in water until ready to prepare. If you don't have a large aquarium for them to swim in (and why would you, since they're only going to be there until dinnertime?), the bathtub will do.

Step 3: Collect the tools you will need. A heavy wooden chopping block that you will never use again. An ice pick. A sharp, heavy cleaver.

Get a nice bottle of Chianti and the biggest wineglass you can find. You're going to need fortification. In fact, it's probably wise to have more than one bottle on hand.

> Step 4: Go get the first eel. Note: When eels feel threatened, they secrete slime. You'll need a rough towel or a heavy glove to provide enough traction to get a good hold on them.

> Step 5: Bring the eel to the kitchen and slap its head down on the chopping block. Try to use enough force to stun him for a second so you can grab your ice pick and drive it through his head to secure him to the chopping block so that you can cut him into pieces. Note: The back end of the eel will wrap itself around your arm like a constrictor and will continue to tighten even after you've whacked its head off. Also, as the blood begins to spurt, the whole situation will become even more slippery.

> Step 6: Unwind the headless eel from your arm and cut it into three-inch sections with your cleaver. Don't become alarmed when the pieces continue to move and the head that is secured to the chopping block with the ice pick squeaks as it gasps for air. This is perfectly normal and means that you have a healthy eel that won't give you botulism or salmonella or whatever it is that you might get from seafood to make you ill.

> Step 7: Repeat process until no eels remain in bathtub and your kitchen looks like the Colos-

seum after a particularly grisly gladiatorial competition.

Step 8: Throw screaming eel heads in garbage.

Step 9: Slice open eel sections and gut them.

Hungry yet?

Step 10: Toss your snake bits into a big bowl of cold water and keep in refrigerator until ready to cook.

Now, here's the easy part:

Step 11: Whip up a couple of eggs. Dip the eel pieces into the eggs, then dredge them in flour that has been seasoned with salt and pepper and fry them in olive oil.

And here's the best part:

Serve to horrified dinner guests.

It was a grand tradition. But after my grandfather died, it went by the wayside for a couple of years.

After we moved into our suburban palazzo, my father decided it was time to pay homage to the gods of good fortune once again and reintroduced eel to the Christmas Eve menu.

This was, without question, the most memorable Christmas of my life.

It began, as most things do in an Italian family, as a great battle.

While both my father and my Uncle Gene agreed that we should have eel on the Christmas Eve menu, neither one of them was prepared to do the dirty work. At the outset, this posed no problem whatsoever, as the man of the house was never expected to do anything that might be even remotely interpreted as "dirty work."

The problems began when my mother—the lady with the biggest set of *coglioni* this side of Naples—refused to do what they were not man enough to even contemplate. She was not unreasonable. She would cook the eels, she told them. But that was as far as she was prepared to go. Meet 'em and eat 'em was simply not on her agenda.

"Well then, I guess it's up to you, Gino," my father told his younger brother.

Uncle Gene just laughed in his face.

"What, are you scared?" my father taunted him.

On the surface, that statement was utterly idiotic. My Uncle Gene was the toughest guy in the universe. A raised eyebrow from him could empty a bar in a matter of seconds. There wasn't a man alive who was a match for Uncle Gene. But "creepy-crawleys" left him paralyzed with fear.

The only one more likely to cry like a little girl at the sight of something icky was my father. So there they were, at an impasse. My father, the older and more weasely of the two—he was after all the lawyer—proposed a solution. If Uncle Gene would drive to Philadelphia to buy the live eels, my father would take it from there.

I was nine years old and I saw the con he was trying to work. "Take it from there" did not mean he was willing to kill the eels himself. All it meant was that while Uncle Gene was

gone he would be busy trying to figure out how to bully someone else into doing it.

He offered me fifty bucks.

I would have done anything for my father, even without the
incentive of cold, hard cash. But I drew the line at killing.

Apparently, so did Uncle Gene.

He returned from Philadelphia in half the time it should
have taken. We knew he was back even before he blew the horn
in the driveway. We'd heard the tires screech as he turned onto
the street. He was barely out of the car when my father and I
ran outside to greet him.

"Your snakes are in the trunk," Uncle Gene said, tossing my
father the car keys.

"Good job," my father said, congratulating him, trying to
butter him up for the next phase of the plan he'd concocted.

My father opened the trunk while Uncle Gene stood back.
Inside there were two brown bags, the tops of which were rolled
down about a third of the way. My father opened one and
peered inside.

"These eels are no good," he announced. "They're already
dead."

It is very dangerous to eat eels that aren't guaranteed to be
perfectly fresh.

"They're not dead," Uncle Gene assured us. "Just stunned."
He went on to explain. "I was not about to drive all the way
back from Philly with a trunk full of wriggling snakes, even if
they were in bags. So before I put them in the trunk, I smacked
the bags up against the side of the car a couple of times just to
knock them out for the ride. Better for them. Better for me."

Turns out he actually did kill about half of them. But there
were still over a dozen that needed killing. And my father was
not about to allow Uncle Gene to leave the premises until that
was done. Especially since my mother had already fled with my

two sisters. They were out doing "last-minute errands" like going to the bakery and anywhere else my mother could think of until she was pretty sure the eel situation was under control. I was invited to go along, but I opted to stay home with the big boys.

Meanwhile, the big boys were getting ready to start throwing punches over who was going to kill our dinner.

As usual, Uncle Gene caved first. He would kill the eels. But only on one condition. If he was going to kill the eels, he was going to do it his way. He would take the eels out into the backyard and shoot them.

I couldn't have imagined a worse idea. But apparently my father did. The thought of his having to kill the eels himself removed all trepidation about Uncle Gene's harebrained scheme. They left me to watch over the bags of eels while they went inside to get the gun.

By the time they came back out, they were engaged in a new argument. Who was the better shot? All of a sudden both of them were hot to kill eels—as long as neither one of them actually had to touch one.

I was beginning to wish I had gone to the bakery with my mother.

"I'm going in the house," I announced. I hated guns, refused to be anywhere near one. But my father collected guns. And though he had some beautiful antiques mounted in glass cases on his office wall, nothing he said or did could make me share his fascination with them, especially the ones that still worked.

Both my father and Uncle Gene had permits. Both practiced regularly on the police firing range. And both should have been poster boys for gun control laws.

They had learned absolutely nothing at all from the last time one of them had tried to solve a problem with a gun. Uncle Gene was home alone one night when he discovered that he had a mouse in the basement—another icky creature that he didn't dare touch. He got the gun and waited patiently for the mouse to show himself. As the vermin scampered out from behind some boxes, Uncle Gene took careful aim. He followed the mouse up the wall and halfway across the ceiling until he was sure he could take him. He fired. The mouse dropped off the ceiling . . . and ran across the floor, right over Uncle Gene's toes, without a scratch on him. The bullet went through the basement ceiling, out the kitchen floor, and blew up the refrigerator.

And now they were about to start shooting eels in the backyard.

While I didn't want to be anywhere near the action, I wasn't about to miss it either. I knew I would be required to testify later when my mother came home and demanded an explanation for the disaster that was sure to greet her.

My bedroom window had a great view of the backyard. I watched as my father and Uncle Gene trekked all the way to the back of the property, which was bordered by pretty dense woods. My father was carrying a bag of eels in one hand and the gun in the other. That left Uncle Gene free to gesticulate dramatically while continuing to argue that he should be the shooter.

My father gave in and handed over the gun. Then he gingerly unrolled the top of the brown bag, picked it up by the bottom corner, shook out the eels, and jumped back.

Uncle Gene never got off a shot.

While the dead eels just landed on the ground with a splat, the live ones slithered off into the woods with lightning speed.

The number of eels available for Christmas Eve dinner was cut in half once again. My father felt his good fortune slipping away from him and he was not happy. As his argument with his brother escalated, I decided it was best if I just stayed in my room. Nonetheless, because of the volume of their voices, I had a very complete oral report of everything that happened.

First, my father insisted that they had to get the rest of the live eels into water before they lost any more of them. But while Tweedledum and Tweedledumber were dumping the eels into the washtub in the basement, three more managed to slip away. Right down the drain. That was when they decided to relocate to my mother's bathroom.

She came home just in time to find half a dozen black, slimy eels swimming happily in her bathtub.

That was when the screaming really began.

Cross-country killing sprees have been accomplished with less drama than it took to get our dinner on the table that night.

In the end, my father did it. He killed the eels. And my mother, ever true to her word, cooked them to perfection.

There were so many people crammed into our dining room that Christmas, it looked like a state dinner. There were aunts and uncles and cousins, most of whom were not related by blood but by culture and deep, abiding friendship. There were our New World friends, who were mostly people my father had met in business. They didn't look like us, or talk like us, or eat like us—but they wanted to. And they were welcomed to our celebration as warmly as if they had been blood relations. It was Christmas after all.

My mother would have happily invited the general public to Christmas Eve dinner if only her table had been a little bigger. As it was, we were all packed in pretty tightly.

The table was set with my mother's best linen, on which she'd laid out the Christmas china with the holly design around the rims of the plates. The silver had been polished until it was positively blinding. And the crystal sparkled in the warm glow of candlelight. As always, there was more than enough food to go around.

We groaned with delight as each new course was presented. And my mother proudly accepted well-deserved compliments on her culinary expertise.

By the time the eels got to the table, the crowd was in a feeding frenzy. And, judging by the Chianti consumption, they were at least as well lit as the dining room. Our poor, unsuspecting dinner guests were heaping their plates with what I am sure they thought was fried chicken, because that's exactly what well-prepared eel looks like.

I chuckled to myself as the serving plate was passed to me and I passed it right along without helping myself to any of its contents.

"What are you doing?" my father asked, as if I'd committed some unspeakable act.

"Passing the dish," I told him.

"Aren't you going to have some?" It was more a command than a question.

"No, thank you," I said, most politely.

"You want to bring bad luck on this family?" he threatened.

"I thought I already had," I said.

"Don't be a wise guy," my father told me. "Take a piece of the eel."

"The what!?" the lovely blond woman sitting next to me gasped, nearly dropping the plate that I had just handed to her. She was the wife of a young lawyer my father had recently hired. She was trying so hard to make a good impression. I couldn't wait to see just how far she would go.

"Eel," my father told her matter-of-factly, as if they were common as dinner rolls. "Take one."

She hesitated.

Her husband glared at her from across the table.

With all eyes on her, she scanned the plate for the smallest piece she could find. As she speared it with her fork, she had the same look of determination and revulsion that my father had had earlier when he drove the ice pick into its head. Then she passed the plate like a little kid playing Hot Potato.

"Taste it," my father instructed.

Her eyes darted around the table, begging for someone to intercede.

I was probably the only person at that table who might be inclined to mouth off to my father. But since the eel plate had passed me by without my having taken a piece, I was in no mood to draw attention to myself.

"You'll like it," he assured her. "It tastes just like chicken."

The poor woman was visibly fighting the gag reflex as she picked up her piece of eel and took a mouse-size nibble off the corner.

"Well?" My father waited for her opinion.

"You're right," she said with a forced smile, putting the eel onto her plate so that it didn't touch any of the other food. "It does taste like chicken."

Under my father's watchful eye, every person at the table took at least one bite of eel, even me. And every one of us, without exception, agreed that it did indeed taste exactly like chicken.

While people in other households were probably recounting the story of the nativity on that most holy night, our whole house was vibrating with laughter from the telling of the tale of the Christmas eels.

On one hand, it did seem pretty stupid to go to all that trouble for something that tasted like chicken. But somehow, amid all the laughter, it was impossible not to feel very, very lucky.

Chapter 9

An Italian Nose

I'D BARELY had enough time to adjust to the brave new world of suburbia when I was beset by even more cataclysmic changes.

It took only a few hysterical outbursts for my mother to realize what was happening. It was then that she presented me with the "little blue book" that was supposed to be my guide through the land mine–riddled path from puberty to young womanhood. Since this was a journey I had no intention of making, I promptly threw the book into the garbage.

And I was not the only one in deep denial over this.

It was increasingly difficult to hide what I was becoming. It may not have been as blatant and dramatic a change as the guy who turned into a werewolf, but it certainly was more frightening to my father. He couldn't quite put his finger on it, couldn't define exactly what it was; but there was something wrong with his kid.

His quest to unravel the mystery began one night at dinner. It was just a typical night. The meal started with the standard ritual. Whereas most people just said grace before eating, we waited with bated breath as my father took the first taste and then proceeded to critique the food. While my father would be the first person to say that my mother was the best cook in the world, he never sat down at the table without finding something wrong. The sauce was too watery. The meat was too dry. It was too salty, or not salted enough.

That night we had beans and escarole—which my father (and many other people of southern Italian origin) pronounced shka-role-eh, rolling the r. It is a simple, hearty, peasant dish that has always been one of my favorites. Like most peasant food, what it lacks in expensive ingredients is made up for by the time and labor required to prepare it properly.

Beans and Escarole
(Fagioli e Scarola)

Step 1: Get a nice big bottle of Chianti. Note: There is no wine in the recipe itself. The wine goes into the cook, not the pot. But somehow it never fails to make the dish taste better—at least to the cook.

Step 2: Get a pot that is nearly large enough to bathe in, one pound of dried red kidney beans, four to six heads of escarole, and about a third of a pound of salt pork. Note: Salt pork is sometimes labeled "fatback." What you want is a piece that is all fat, no meat, and pretty heavily salted.

Step 3: Wash the beans and put them into the pot. Cover with two to three inches of water and put it on a low flame with the lid of the pot tilted just enough for steam to escape.

Step 4: Chop the salt pork until it is almost the consistency of butter. Before the invention of the Cuisinart my mother did this using a chopping block and a cleaver. She would heat the blade over one of the gas burners on the stove, then chop away until the blade needed to be reheated. It took a long time and a lot of energy to get the job done that way.

Step 5: Add the chopped salt pork to the pot with the beans and continue to simmer for two to three hours. The liquid should become rather thick, more like stew than soup. Taste, and add salt if needed.

Step 6: Wash and dry the escarole. This is not as easy as it sounds, as escarole is a particularly dirty vegetable. The best way to accomplish the task is to fill the sink with water and soak the leaves. Remove the leaves to dry one at a time, giving them an extra rinse as needed.

Step 7: Add the escarole to the pot in large handfuls. Stir after each handful until the leaves begin to wilt and mix in with the beans, otherwise the weight of the escarole will burn the beans on the bottom of the pot.

Step 8: After all the escarole is blended in, cover and continue to simmer for at least another half hour.

Step 9: Serve in large soup bowls with lots of crusty bread.

With a meal like this in front of me, I had no intention of waiting for my father's opinion. I dug right in.

"The shkarole is a little bitter," my father proclaimed after his first bite.

My mother just shook her head, bemused by him as always. "Not my fault," she told him. "I didn't grow it."

"Yeah, but you've got to learn how to pick good vegetables," he said.

They'd had this conversation before when my father had insisted that his veal was too tough. It ended with him deciding that he should accompany her on her next food-shopping excursion in order to teach her how to pick a good piece of meat. As it turned out, he did have very specific criteria. He looked through all the packages and took the ones with the highest prices. In his mind, the exorbitant price must, after all, mean something. Of course it did; it meant that you were getting a lot more meat by weight.

We ended up with enough meat for a month. And during that time my father raved about the meals my mother prepared. "Is this the meat I bought?" he'd ask before he tasted it. After my mother answered that it was, he commented favorably on every bite. He even toyed with the idea of doing the shopping with my mother all the time. But somehow she managed to avoid that. She preferred to endure his criticism at the table rather than endure the embarrassment of having the grocery clerk ask her if they were building a bomb shelter.

"Baby, don't you think the shkarole is bitter?" he asked me.

"Nope," I answered, shoveling in another mouthful. I thought it was delicious.

"It must be me," he said with a shrug. "I must be going crazy."

"Must be," I agreed with a chuckle.

"Baby, why do you always pick on me?"

" 'Cause I'm a rotten kid," I answered.

"I'll say," my sister piped up. "And ugly too."

"Don't say that," my father scolded. "Your sister is beautiful."

My sister rolled her eyes and so did I.

I shouldn't have done that. I should have learned to agree with my father no matter what he said. That one little look ended up costing me months of heartache. That look said to my father that I was displeased about my appearance, that I felt there was something about me that wasn't quite right. He'd been feeling that too.

I watched him stare at me and then lean back in his chair the way he did whenever he was sure he had the answer. It had obviously dawned on him what was wrong. It was as plain as . . .

"Baby, tell me something," he said to me. "How do you feel about your nose?"

I wrinkled my brow. He could tell that I was really considering this question. And I was. "Fine, I guess," I said cautiously, trying to figure out exactly where this conversation was headed. "It works all right." After all, I could smell trouble in the air.

"No," he said. "I'm talking about the way it looks."

"Well, it looks like a nose. And I guess I'm happy about that. I'd probably feel pretty awful if I had an ear there."

"Aw, Baby, you don't have to hide your feelings by joking about them." He was getting sensitive. The evening was sure to turn into a disaster. "I know you're a little embarrassed about your nose. I felt the same way when I was your age. Believe me, I understand how important this is to you. And that's why we're going to get it fixed."

"What?!"

"You don't have to be afraid. It's really very simple. They put you to sleep and the doctor just takes a little piece off your nose right here." He ran his finger down his own nose to demonstrate. "And then your nose will be perfect. It'll look just like this." He put his finger on the tip of his nose and pushed it up a little.

"I don't want to look like Porky Pig," I protested. I looked to my mother to intercede, but she was too dumbfounded to speak.

"You won't look like Porky Pig," my father insisted. "They'll do a good job and you'll look great. And then you won't have to go through life feeling self-conscious about having a big Guinea nose the way I have."

I hadn't been self-conscious about my nose, hadn't ever even really given it much thought—until then. Feeling both insulted and threatened, the specter of an operation looming large, I went on the offensive. "If you're so upset about your nose, why don't *you* have a nose job?" I suggested none too delicately.

"I don't need one," he shot back.

"Your nose is bigger than mine," I said, hitting below the belt.

"Is it really that bad?" He turned his head so that we could all examine his profile.

"Your nose is fine," we all agreed. It was a classic Roman nose, the same kind of nose that's on every marble bust of every Caesar in every museum in the world. It was a nose that was good enough for emperors but somehow not good enough for my father.

"I'm just saying," I continued, defending my position and my nose, "if you don't need a nose job—and you don't—then I don't need one either." Hormonal hysteria was creeping into my voice.

Plain old Italian hysteria got the better of him. "It's too late for me. But you're still young. I am not going to allow you to go through life feeling the way I did."

"Don't holler at me," I shouted, holding back tears.

"I am not hollering." He was hollering. "This is the way I talk." It was the way he talked a lot of the time. "And if you don't like it, that's just too bad." Nobody liked it. And he knew it. Still, more often than not, it was one of the tools he employed to get his own way. "Now, you need a nose job. And you're going to have one. And you ought to be grateful that you have an old man who can afford to do that for you."

"Thanks a lot," I said sarcastically. "If you've got so much money to throw around, I'd be a lot happier if you bought me a horse instead of hiring somebody to cut me up like Frankenstein."

"Don't be so dramatic," he told me. My father never really got that old adage about the pot and the kettle. "I'm only doing this because I love you."

"Well you know what?" I said, getting up from the table. "I hate you. And I don't ever want to talk to you again!" With that, I burst into tears and ran upstairs to my room.

I headed straight for the mirror of the dresser and stood in front of it, staring at myself for a long time. I tilted my head in every direction and strained my eyes, trying to get a good look at my profile. No matter how hard I looked, I could find nothing wrong with my nose, certainly nothing that would require an operation.

After a while, I got bored with my nose. But I never seemed

to tire of the opportunity to wallow in self-pity. It was an excellent sport. And I'd learned it from the master.

I found myself transfixed by my image in the mirror. It was such a perfectly tragic picture that it made me cry. As the tears welled up in my eyes, my reflection became blurry. I tilted my head and saw the little pool shift to the corners of my eyes without spilling. I tilted my head the other way and felt the tears wash across my eyeballs and come to rest on the other side, still not spilling a drop. It was an interesting sensation and I fought the urge to blink so that I could study it some more.

I was leaning in close to the mirror, watching the tears move as I tilted my head back and forth, when my mother came into the room. She didn't bother to ask what I was doing, but she did respond to the tears.

"Don't worry, you're not going to have a nose job," she assured me. "You don't need one. Your nose is perfect just the way it is. And Daddy didn't mean to hurt your feelings. He's just . . ." She trailed off, unable to explain whatever it was that went on in his head.

"You promise you won't let him make me get a nose job?"

"Yes," she said. "I promise."

My mother's promise was more binding than a contract signed in blood. My nose was safe. My psyche, however, was another matter.

"Now why don't you come downstairs and finish your dinner," she suggested.

"I'm not going back down there unless he apologizes," I told her.

She almost laughed.

I knew I was asking the impossible. My father did not know how to apologize. He was a lawyer through and through. He could justify. He could rationalize. He could lie to your face without flinching. But apologize? Never.

"How about if I bring your dinner up here?"

"Good idea," I agreed.

I ate my dinner, finished my homework, and went to bed, enjoying the solitude and wondering if there wasn't some way to extend it for at least a few days.

It was still dark when he came into my room. He shook my leg until I opened my eyes.

I had the sensation of falling and my body jerked under the covers. I was sure I had just tumbled from one dream into another.

My father was standing in front of me, just a shadow in the dark room. Then he began to speak. "I'm going to the hospital now," he said calmly and very coolly, so coolly in fact that I could almost see his breath in the air. "By the time you wake up, you'll have your wish. You'll never have to speak to me again. Because I will be dead."

He turned and walked away.

I rolled over in search of a better dream. And I must have gotten one because I slept right through the ringing of my alarm clock, and my mother had to wake me to get ready for school. As I got out of bed, the strange dream came flooding back to me. "Mom," I said as she was heading out the door. "Daddy's not dead, is he?"

She started to laugh, an odd reaction I thought. "Why do you ask?" she wanted to know.

"I had the strangest dream last night," I told her. "I dreamt that Daddy was here and he said that he was going to the hospital to die."

"That wasn't a dream," she said, still laughing. "He did go to the hospital last night."

"You're kidding." I was suddenly filled with terror and, worse yet, guilt.

"He's fine," she assured me.

"Then why did he have to go to the hospital?" Even he wouldn't go to those extremes just to make me feel guilty.

"He thought he was having a heart attack," she explained. "But it turns out it wasn't a heart attack at all. You see, after you left the table last night, your father finished off the whole pot of beans and escarole."

The way my mother cooked, that was roughly enough beans and escarole to feed a medium-size Italian village. Nothing was ever done in moderation in our house.

"Then he laid down on the couch and went to sleep," she continued. "He woke up at about three o'clock in the morning, writhing in pain, and insisting that he had to go to the hospital because he was dying. And I think he was actually a little disappointed when the doctor assured him that he wasn't."

"So what was wrong with him?"

"He had gas." She started laughing again. "I guess that'll teach him to eat a whole pot of beans and escarole all by himself."

It didn't. He kept right on doing it. He just didn't go to the hospital afterward.

He also kept bring up the subject of a nose job from time to time. And despite the fact that I knew my mother would never allow it, I did begin worrying about my nose. I charted its growth in the mirror every day. And whenever I sat with my chin resting in the palm of my hand, I'd keep my index finger up under my nose, pushing it up, hoping that it would grow that way.

In the meantime, my father also decided that I needed braces so that my teeth wouldn't stick out. Luckily, the orthodontist convinced him that I didn't need braces. Then he was back to more plastic surgery. Suddenly, my ears became a problem. He was afraid that they stuck out like his. His ears were fine, but I walked around feeling like Dumbo. I started combing my hair over my ears so that nobody could see them and before too long he forgot all about them.

Finally he gave up altogether. He resigned himself to the fact that what was troubling him couldn't be changed. What was making me less than perfect wasn't my nose or my teeth or my ears that stuck out. It was my newly acquired B cups.

Chapter 10

⤜❧⤛

Broad-Minded

IN THE grand scheme of things, my breasts turned out to be a relatively small problem. It took much bigger breasts than mine to create real pandemonium in our household.

They arrived one Saturday when my parents were having a big old-fashioned, all-American backyard barbecue for just about everyone they'd ever met.

Two great big boobs arrived in an Aston Martin, which pulled up right in front of our house.

The one in the driver's seat was Broadway Joe. No, he was not the famous quarterback for the New York Jets. He was just a local playboy who'd laid claim to the glamorous moniker by virtue of the fact that he kept an apartment in Manhattan where he could entertain his "lady friends."

Which brings us to the other boob, or pair thereof, the "lady friend." Her name was Kitty, or Bambi, or Thumper. I don't think anyone ever really got it straight except to know that it was some furry creature. The reason that no one could manage to keep their wits about them was because this particular piece of fluff had decided that the perfect attire for a picnic was a tight black leather miniskirt and a see-through top—both *sans* undergarments.

"Get rid of them," my mother hissed at my father as she pulled me away from the kitchen window where I'd been watching the men swarm around the bimbo like mosquitoes drawn to a bug zapper.

"They're our guests," my father protested. "We can't be rude."

"Rude?" I practically shrieked, reclaiming my position at the window. I couldn't help myself, but I was drawn to the scene like a gawker at a train wreck. "Maybe you haven't noticed, but that broad out there came to Mommy's party half-naked. Don't you think she's the one who's a little rude?"

This time it was my father who pulled me away from the window.

My mother just rolled her eyes and shrugged her shoulders and said, "Out of the mouths of babes!"

What surprised me was not that she had agreed with me, but that she hadn't objected to my use of the word *broad*. It was a word my mother hated, and one my father used regularly. But I think that at that moment in time, we all three recognized and accepted the fact that I had added a new word to my vocabulary and had used it in a sentence properly. There was simply no other way to describe the buxom, bleached-blond creature who had taken up her position on the patio right in front of the giant, silver champagne fountain, acting twice as bubbly as a case of Piper Heidsieck.

"Please don't make a scene," my father implored my mother.

Again I opened my mouth to point out the obvious.

But this time they both shot me a warning look. I was standing between a keg of dynamite and a match; no need to spew fuel. A long and painful silence ensued as I shoved my hand under my chin to hold my mouth shut tight.

"So what would you like me to do?" my mother asked my father, her tone as haughty as a queen's.

Yet I couldn't help but notice that she was still deferring to the king.

I pressed my hand harder against my chin.

"Just ignore her," he said, finding the easiest possible way out.

"Can you?" she shot back.

He tried. And failed, right along with every other male guest at the picnic.

My mother, my aunts, and all their women friends tried too. Within minutes, they'd brought *their* party into the house. There was enough food and drink left in the kitchen that none of them had to venture outside again for any reason. And none of them did.

Nor did any of the men venture inside.

I'd never seen such a polarization of the sexes.

"So I hear she's a real 'bunny,' " one of my aunts said as she reached into the refrigerator and pulled out a bottle of champagne.

"Oh really?" another one retorted. "I thought the word was 'pussy.' "

They all laughed. But not really. What was so funny after all?

Outside, holding court, was a woman who made her living as

a *Playboy* bunny. She served drinks wearing a headband that sprouted rabbit ears and little else but a cotton ball glued to her butt.

While inside, there were women who'd worked hard all their lives to overcome a stereotype. They'd worked against all odds, against a lack of funds, a lack of access to formal education, and a lack of moral support. They'd worked, many times in menial jobs, to put their husbands through school so that, as a family, they could realize the American Dream—if not for themselves, then certainly for their children. And on the surface, it looked as if they had succeeded.

Our backyard was full of doctors and lawyers and accomplished businessmen. And it was all thanks to the hardworking women who were holed up in the kitchen, the women who made it a point to be well read, well spoken, and well dressed— despite the fact that by accident of birth they had probably never been referred to as well bred.

But while they were working so hard against the ethnic machismo that kept them down, they found themselves blindsided by the all-American *Playboy* mentality that took its place.

That evening was one giant disaster. Instead of the sprawling lawn party my mother had envisioned, the women closed ranks in the kitchen. And just like soldiers who have retreated to the bunker, they tried to make the best of it. They talked one another through, sharing everything from the latest recipes in the women's magazines to their oft-repeated stories of the horrors of childbirth.

It was their graphic descriptions of the rigors and pains of labor whose only relief was passing something the size of a watermelon through a space that seemed in no way designed to accommodate such a thing that finally caused me to seek refuge in the privacy of my own room. But as I listened to them laugh, I realized that in so many ways they were tougher than soldiers in a bunker. They were certainly tougher than I would ever be. They were certainly tougher than any of the well-educated professionals who were laughing outside, trying to charm the one woman who'd done nothing more to earn their attention than to give them a peep show.

The laughter ended early that evening, much earlier than it ever had before when my parents had thrown a party. In the end, nobody could really ignore the white elephant.

After everyone had gone, I sat at the top of the stairs and listened to my parents argue as my mother shoveled pounds of leftover shrimp and all the other delicacies that she'd bought and prepared so lovingly into garbage bags.

My mother never threw away good food. It was clear that she just wanted to be rid of every trace of the evening's fiasco.

To that end, she probably should have stuffed my father into one of her big green bags. It probably took all of her self-control not to do just that, especially after he opened his mouth.

"She was actually a nice girl," my father said defensively. He was not defending the bimbo. In truth, he really couldn't have cared less about her. It was his own stupid behavior that he was defending, as well as the behavior of the rest of the pack of wolves he'd been hunting with.

"Really?" My mother's tone made the word *sarcasm* seem like a warm and fuzzy lesson for the day on *Sesame Street*.

"Maybe if you had been open-minded enough to see past the clothes she was wearing, you would have found something about her that you liked."

"Well you should know," she said, "since you were looking right past her clothes to see exactly what it was that you liked."

"She was an interesting person," my father rebutted, trying to affect a tone of righteous indignation.

"She was a dumb 'bunny,'" my mother said flatly, but very, very loudly.

"Not so dumb," he shot back in his cold, courtroom voice. I knew right away that this was going to get really ugly. "Did you see that car they drove up in?"

She didn't bother to answer. She just kept slamming things around the kitchen.

He went on. "It was hers. He bought it for her birthday. She has a great apartment in Manhattan. He pays the rent. She eats at all the best restaurants, never picks up a bill. She's traveled all over the world." My father was clearly in awe, sounding a little envious even. I didn't get the impression that he wanted to be the dope who was paying for everything; I got the feeling that the one he envied was the tart.

"And your point is?" my mother said. I could tell by her voice that it wasn't so much because she really wanted to know, but because she really wanted him to stop before he did any more damage.

"Just that she's not so dumb." It was probably the worst summation he'd ever given in his entire life.

There was a pregnant pause before the prosecution took the floor and proceeded to tear him to shreds. "So a smart woman is one who never has to foot the bill?"

He had to be argumentative. It was in his nature. "Yeah," he retorted. "A smart woman can buy a one-way plane ticket to anywhere in the world and never have to spend another penny."

"Well, I guess that makes me a real idiot."

This time, thankfully, there was no answer.

"Because I suppose that if I were a smart woman," my mother went on, "I would be well acquainted with all the ceilings in all the hotel rooms in all the world too. Silly me! I just always thought that if I worked hard enough, I'd be able to see so much more."

With no other line of defense available to him, my father resorted to an old favorite. "You're a real ball-breaker."

I'd learned that in my father's mind, women were divided into two categories. There were the women who worked hard and expected some degree of remuneration and respect for all that they did. And for some reason, that made them "ballbreakers." Then there were the ones who picked your pocket while they flashed their assets. Those were "bimbos."

What I couldn't figure out was why men always seemed to gravitate to the bimbos.

My mother seemed to be equally perplexed by that question. "Why are men so stupid?"

It was a rhetorical question. Nonetheless, he felt compelled to answer it. "I resent that," he said, as if he were in a courtroom making an objection.

His objection was quickly overruled.

"Do you want to know what I resent?" the judge, jury, and executioner retorted. "I resent the fact that you have three daughters and yet you have made no attempt to understand the lives of women. I resent the fact that you can stand here and tell me that a woman who has nothing else to recommend her but an astonishing pair of tits—which were also bought and paid for by your friend—is a 'smart woman.' Is that the kind of 'smart woman' you want to see your daughters grow up to be? Is that the kind of life you want for them?"

Case closed.

My mother stormed out of the kitchen before he could say another word. She left him alone to figure it out for himself.

As I retreated into my own room so that I wouldn't be caught eavesdropping, I couldn't help thinking that while my mother really was a smart woman, she never seemed to learn that letting him figure things out for himself was the worst thing she could possibly do.

Chapter 11

Breakin' Balls

AFTER GIVING it an awful lot of thought, my father finally realized that he had no choice but to accept the fact that his kid was not going to grow up to be a "real man." But neither would he allow his kid to grow up to be "some dippy broad." What I was going to have to become in order to please my father was "as good as a man."

There were things implicit in that attitude that I should have found offensive. But I didn't. I was young and foolish, and at the time, a lot of other women were erroneously adopting that very same attitude. I bought in without any reservations whatsoever. I found the idea of being "as good as a man" perfectly thrilling. To me it meant that I could be more concerned with the measurement of my IQ than with my bust size. And it gave me license to be good at things other than cooking or cleaning.

I was more than just a little envious of the things for which grown men were well rewarded. I was appalled by the fact that sports stars were paid exorbitant amounts of money just to play the same games they had enjoyed in childhood.

I'd never played baseball again after having been disqualified from the game on the basis that I was a girl. I refused even to watch it on television. And I'd turned my back on all other organized sports as well, much to my father's dismay.

But when I was about thirteen years old, there suddenly and quite serendipitously appeared a game that broke down the barriers between me and the testosterone club. And this time I wasn't playing with little boys. This was a game that I played with grown men—for money.

One day, to my mother's great surprise and even greater chagrin, a pool table was delivered to our house. It was a "gift" from one of my father's clients for a job well done. My mother had the "delivery men" put it down in the basement.

From the moment it arrived, my father and I spent every free moment we had down in that basement learning the game. All it really took was a steady hand, a keen eye for spatial relationships, and lots and lots of practice.

Because I had much more free time on my hands than my father did, I quickly excelled. I got to the point where I could hit a cue ball with such accuracy that I could send it the length of the table to kiss a ball resting on the opposite cushion with just enough force to make that ball roll two feet, hugging the cushion all the way, and drop gently into the pocket.

It made my father proud. And while he hated the fact that I beat him regularly, and usually pretty badly, he was quick to see opportunity in the situation. His little girl was going to become a big-time hustler.

Our basement became a social club.

Only my father and Uncle Gene were allowed to know how good I was. In front of everyone else, I was supposed to play dumb.

On any given night, my father would invite a group of guys over to the house to shoot pool. But somehow, he'd always be short one guy. They'd never realize that error until after they'd all had a few drinks and were already down in the basement ready to go. What to do?

"Well, my kid shoots a pretty good game of pool," I'd hear my father say as I stood at the top of the basement steps waiting for my cue to enter. "I'll just go upstairs and get her."

Since my father was pretty sure that none of his other guests would be ill mannered enough to say what he was actually thinking, that job fell to Uncle Gene.

"Aw, geez," Uncle Gene would groan as I clomped, none too gracefully, down the basement steps behind my father. "How are we supposed to shoot pool with a little girl down here? Now what? I gotta watch my language?" He'd make sure that no one was watching him before he'd shoot me a wink.

"You never watch your language, Uncle Gene," I'd answer, trying to sneak in a wink of my own. "Besides, what am I going to hear that I haven't heard before?" That always got a laugh from any guests who were as well acquainted with my father's and Uncle Gene's four-letter vocabulary as I was.

Uncle Gene would parry by saying, "I guess this means we can't smoke or drink while we play either."

"Why not?" I'd shoot back. "I'm usually the one who empties your ashtrays and refills your drinks."

That always got another laugh.

Unbeknownst to them, Uncle Gene had set me up to show off my balls.

It worked. The other guys always decided that I ought to be allowed to stay. But none of them was magnanimous enough to offer to be my partner.

I was the last kid on the playground to be picked. And poor, old Uncle Gene was always the one who got stuck with me. It seemed like poetic justice to everyone else, since he had been the complainer.

Too bad they didn't really know anything about me and Uncle Gene.

Uncle Gene was my best buddy, my longtime partner in crime.

When I was born, he was only sixteen years old. While it may have been considered unmanly at that time for boys to play with dolls, having a real baby to dote on was a whole different story.

Uncle Gene spoiled me rotten, worse even than my grandfather. The six of us—my grandparents and Uncle Gene, and my parents and I—all lived together in our little three-bedroom, one-bath, semidetached house. While Uncle Gene may have been the lowest man in the chain of command, he was also the one who never let me down.

Here's how it usually went.

"Mommy, can I have . . . ?" It didn't matter exactly what it was I wanted. That usually changed from day to day, if not minute to minute.

"No."

"Daddy, can I have . . . ?"

"What did your mother say?"

"No."

"Then I guess the answer is no."

"Grandmom, can I have . . . ?"

"No."

"Grandpop, can I have . . . ?"

"What did your grandmother say?"

"No."

"Then the answer is no."

"Uncle Gene."

"What do you want, kiddo?"

Bingo! Uncle Gene never said no. Somehow he always found a way to get me whatever it was I wanted.

It was Uncle Gene who got me my first puppy. It happened one day when everybody else was out and Uncle Gene was left to take care of me. I told him I wanted a puppy. So he found an ad in the newspaper for free puppies. He made a phone call, put me in the car, took me to a place where I got to take my pick of a litter of ten German shepherd puppies, and he even let me name it.

By the time we got home with "Duke," everybody else had returned. They'd already worked themselves into quite a panic after coming home to an empty house. But the sight of the puppy sent them into levels of hysteria I'd never seen before. The hollering in the house got so loud that the vibrations caused the doorbell to start ringing all by itself.

Through it all, there was never any mention of getting rid of the puppy. Not one of them had the heart to take it away from me. There was, however, a great deal of discussion about getting rid of Uncle Gene. It was nothing I hadn't heard before. It was the same scolding he got every time he said yes after everyone else had said no. It never seemed to matter to him.

It mattered to me though. It made him my hero.

And I became his too. Every time he and I destroyed the competition around the pool table, our bond became tighter and tighter.

The ruse worked time and time again because no grown

man would ever accept the fact that a "little girl" had bested him.

While my father never actually threw a game of pool, it didn't really matter to him whether he won or lost. Either way, he and his partner were united in a common cause. That was the real point of the whole exercise. That was what ultimately served his Machiavellian purposes.

The game was never about setting up some stooge in order to take his money. The stakes were always so much higher than that. Besides, in the end my father usually covered his team-mate's losses as well as his own. And Uncle Gene and I always squared up with him after everyone else had gone.

The game was about power.

My father's favorite mark was one of the prosecutors against whom he regularly tried cases and regularly beat. The poor, dumb bastard never understood what hit him. While he was busy trying to keep from losing his money to a "little girl" while shooting pool, he was also shooting off his mouth and giving his case away to her old man.

It seemed to me that my father did more business around that pool table than he did in his office. And I was happy about that, because it worked out really well for me. While I wasn't making anywhere near as much money as he was, I was doing pretty well for myself.

I found that I was comfortable down there in the basement with the smoke, and the booze, and the language, and the power playing. It was so much more fun than being upstairs with cof-fee and fashion and recipes. For the women to like me, I had to be sickeningly polite. For the men to like me, all I had to do was win their money. And I did.

Around the pool table, I was one of them. There was no "Refill my drink while I take my shot, will you, Honey?" Nobody watched his language for my sake. And I was given no special considerations, not even for my height. I wasn't allowed to use the "bridge" to make a shot. "If you can't make the shot without using the 'sissy stick,' you don't make it." Those were the rules. I was happy to abide by them. I was happier still to be "one of the boys."

The only problem was that it was the only social life I had.

It wasn't because we were living in the wasteland I'd imagined when we'd made the move out to the 'burbs. Our neighborhood had really begun to take shape. It was everything my father had promised it would be—lots of great big houses set on large, beautifully landscaped properties. It was the same kind of neighborhood I saw every week on *The Brady Bunch*. And, just like the Bradys, we were pretty much on our own.

Most of the neighbors seemed like nice enough people. They'd smile or wave; and if you passed by them at close enough range, they might even stop to exchange a few pleasant words. But people didn't really become involved with one another, not the way they had in my old neighborhood. It sometimes seemed to me that as more and more houses became occupied, the deeper my own sense of loneliness grew.

This feeling was exacerbated by the fact that there were very few kids my own age who were stuck in the terrible 'tweens—that last interminable year of suffering before being granted entry into that great bastion of coolness, high school. There were families with older teenagers, and families with younger children. The older kids wanted nothing to do with me, and I wanted nothing to do with the younger ones. There were retired couples whose children had grown and gone. And there were a few couples who for various reasons simply had no children.

There were four boys in the neighborhood, from four different families, who were almost exactly my age. They had banded together very quickly and always traveled in a pack, like a litter of clumsy puppies, though nowhere near as cute.

We had not yet reached the stage where boys and girls become obsessed with one another. And if they had any interest whatsoever in girls as a whole, they certainly had none at all in me as an individual. That is, until summer came around and they realized that my family was the only one in the neighborhood that had a built-in swimming pool.

While having a built-in swimming pool is always better than not, sitting beside it all alone has an extremely limited entertainment value. There are simply not enough books in the world to compensate for a lack of human companionship. So when the boys came nosing around for an invitation to go swimming, I was more than happy to oblige.

My backyard became party central. And, to my mother's credit, she never complained about the amount of potato chips, pretzels, and soda I offered to my guests and which they happily consumed. Every once in a while, she'd even throw hot dogs and hamburgers on the grill for everybody.

In addition to the four boys and me, there was always the little rat pack that belonged to my sisters, as well as the only other girl in the neighborhood who was my age and who my mother always forced me to invite for propriety's sake.

Her name was Barbie. It was Barbara actually. But she always introduced herself as "Barbie, like the doll." In fact, she was nothing like the doll. In fact, she had no more hope than I did of ever looking like the doll. She was knock-kneed, and with her mousy brown hair and her slightly crossed eyes, she'd be lucky if she ever even managed to resemble Midge, Barbie's painfully goofy friend.

But she didn't see it that way. As far as she was concerned, she was "Barbie," and quite a doll. As far as I was concerned, her unwavering belief in that said to me that this was a girl with a real set of balls. And on some level, I was forced to admire that.

But on every other level, I really hated her guts. We had nothing in common. While I'd been raised to play with cowboy guns, and swashbuckler swords, and Lincoln Logs, and plastic dinosaur sets, she'd been brought up to be a girly-girl right from the start. And the older she got, the more she valued her makeup bags and nail kits and hairdressing accoutrements and froufrou outfits.

It didn't bother me so much that the only esoteric conversation I could have with this girl was about the wonderful world of nail polish colors. I even tried to be tolerant of the fact that the number of colors she was capable of identifying with any degree of accuracy was fewer than those found in the kindergarten-size crayon box. What did get my knickers in a twist was that in her insatiable desire to be the center of attention—the boys' attention—she found it necessary to demean and embarrass me at every opportunity. In my own backyard, in my own swimming pool, I found myself the object of ridicule.

The boys always laughed when she pointed out the fact that I refused to take off my T-shirt even when I went in the water. They quickly picked up her nickname for me—"no-ass." And they treated my little sisters with even more disdain than they did me.

I endured it all with a smile and a shrug, having convinced myself that this was somehow better than sitting all by myself day after day. But I was painfully aware of the fact that not one of them was there because they enjoyed my company. They were there because summers were long and hot and boring and I had a pool in which to drown those problems. I knew that I was, in effect, trying to buy friendship.

The men with whom I shot pool in the basement paid me more attention and gave me more respect than the boys of summer who'd invaded my backyard. The only time they even feigned any degree of friendship with me was when my mother was at hand.

It didn't take me long to decide that if they were going to

enjoy my hospitality without any voluntary quid pro quo, I would have to find another way to get something for myself out of this equation.

"Want to shoot a game of pool?" I asked ever so innocently one day when the boys had obviously tired of swimming and were threatening to take their beach towels and go home.

Well, that certainly piqued their interest. "You have a pool table?" one of them blurted out, none too coolly.

"Yes," I answered smugly. "It's down in the basement. We have a pinball machine too. So who wants to play?"

The answer was everybody, everybody except Barbie. But she was forced to tag along because her only alternative was to sit beside the pool all alone, as I had done for the first half of the summer.

But the basement was my milieu. And while the boys didn't smoke or drink or swear, they lost their money to me just like men. As a result, I earned their admiration—and Barbie's hatred.

Hell hath no fury like a woman scorned—or a teenage girl ignored. Not only was Barbie never allowed to play, but we also didn't even let her keep score, since she always snuck extra points to whichever boy she happened to fancy on any given day. I should not have been surprised that she quickly devised a way to wreak revenge.

"I just got an interesting phone call," my mother informed me one evening not too long after all my "friends" had left. She hit the word *interesting* with an interesting tone. It was a tone that screamed "trouble."

Show no fear! That was something I'd learned from my father. "Really?" I tried to sound disinterested.

"Yes, really." She was very, very interested. "I just had a long conversation with Barbie's mother."

Oh shit! I thought, but somehow I managed not to say that out loud. In fact, I said nothing, did nothing, refused even to change the blank expression on my face. Oh yeah, I was taking the Fifth on whatever this was going to be about.

But here came the third degree. "Are you, or are you not taking money from boys?" While it was my mother who'd worked to put my father through law school, I was always pretty sure that the money would have been better spent if it had been the other way around. The woman was ruthless.

"What are you talking about?" Answer a question with a question. That way, you're not lying and it gives you time to get your bearings.

"I think you know what I'm talking about." She knew the game as well as I did. Probably better.

Still, I refused to answer on the grounds that . . .

Even without a judge and jury present, my mother played it for all the drama it was worth. "Barbie's mother has just informed me that you have been 'hustling' boys for money." Wow, could that woman emote!

It took all my self-control not to laugh in her face. I knew the word *hustling* meant something very different to her than it did to me. I also knew that once she discovered her error—one that had been propagated first by Barbie, then by her mother—she was going to feel a little silly about it all.

I decided that the truth, while still meeting with great disapproval from my mother, provided me enough safety to have a little fun with the situation. "Yeah," I told her like a perp in cuffs, fessing up, "I hustle boys for money. So what?"

"So what?!" She just about had a heart attack.

With that little bomb I'd dropped on her, I'd very nearly killed my mother. And I couldn't help doubling over with laughter.

She caught on right away. "What are you talking about?" she demanded to know.

"What were *you* talking about?" Always answer a question with a question. It makes them crazy.

But she was still my mother, and if not the highest court in the land, certainly the highest in our house. "You better start explaining," she warned. "And it had better be good."

So I came clean. I confessed to her that I shot pool for money. I did it with boys. And I did it with grown men too.

While I could tell that she was amused, despite the fact that she tried to hide it, she was not happy. "You can't do that," she told me. "It's just not right for a girl to be shooting pool for money."

"Would it be better if I were 'hustling'?" I bristled. Ever since I'd given up baseball, I was overly sensitive to being told that I couldn't or shouldn't do something simply because I was a girl.

My mother understood. "Look, I know it seems stupid to you. And it is stupid. But people talk. And if you keep up this kind of behavior, you'll get a reputation."

"I already have a reputation," I countered. "That's why everybody's willing to put up money to try to beat me."

"Touché," she said, conceding the point, and I think wishing that she could concede the whole game. But she was a product of her generation too, bound by its rules and mores. "I can't let you do it anymore," she half-apologized. "You can still invite the boys over to go swimming if you want to," she said. "You can even shoot pool with them. But there will be no more 'hustling.' Understood?"

I could tell from her tone of voice that this was non-negotiable. I nodded my agreement.

"I mean it," she said, pressing the point. "You are not to shoot pool for money ever again."

"Not even with Daddy and his friends?" I had to ask. I had to take one last stab at being allowed to hold on to my main source of income.

She didn't answer right away. That was a good sign. She was giving the matter some serious consideration. "How often do you win?" she asked finally.

"Almost always," I answered honestly, not even trying to hide my sense of pride in that fact.

She smiled in spite of herself. "Then clean them out," she told me. Once again, my mother let me know that not only did she want me to be able to play with the big boys, she also wanted me to beat them.

≈

Chapter 12

Driving the Cadillac

I WAS THIRTEEN years old when my father decided it was time I learned to drive a car. And not just any old car either, but his brand-spankin'-new, top-of-the-line Cadillac.

As with most of his decisions regarding family life, this one was made without a great deal of forethought, probably ten seconds tops. It was also a decision he made, obviously, without consulting my mother. "Don't tell your mother" was an oft-heard refrain that invariably preceded some ill-advised adventure.

He never had to say that. My dedication to *omertà* was as strict and as sacred as that of any wise guy who ever held the burning holy card while swearing secrecy to La Cosa Nostra—

"this thing of ours." My father and I had our own little Cosa Nostra. It was called: "whatever Mommy doesn't know won't hurt us." We both got away with lots of stuff because of it. But it also brought us very close together.

In a backward sort of way, it taught me that I could depend on my father, no matter what. So when the going got tough, I called Daddy.

There's nothing in the world tougher than going to your first high school dance—all alone.

I was in a brand-new school, one that was not of my own choosing. I had wanted to go to public school, like all the other kids in my "new and improved" neighborhood. But my parents didn't think that was good enough for me. So they chose to send me to an elite, private high school where they were sure that not only would I get the best education possible, but I would also be surrounded by the "best" people.

The school was elite all right, so elite in fact that it didn't take me long to realize that among my peers—many of whom had been together since kindergarten—I was an "untouchable."

I had no desire to go to the dance, no interest in socializing with kids who had done nothing but give me the cold shoulder for close to two months. Unfortunately, I made the mistake of throwing the flyer announcing the dance into the garbage at home instead of trashing it at school the minute I got it.

My mother found it and decided that it was absolutely imperative that I go. She insisted that it would be a wonderful opportunity for me to get to know my schoolmates better under more relaxed circumstances. She reminisced about all the dances she'd gone to in high school and how much fun they were. She wanted me to have all the fun she did as a teenager. She was immune to my protests, assuring me that what I was feeling was perfectly normal, but that my trepidation would dissolve as soon as I hit the dance floor. She even got my father to put the pressure on. "Look, I'll give you a hundred bucks if you go to the stupid dance and make your mother happy. It'll be the easiest hundred bucks you'll ever make in your life. And if you really don't like it when you get there, you call me and I'll come and get you right away."

Against my better judgment, I went—all alone. I hoped that my mother was right. "You're going to have a great time," she assured me once again as she dropped me off in front of the school.

But as I watched her drive away, I had a sick feeling in the pit of my stomach that this was going to be one of those rare occasions when she was dead wrong. I probably would have stayed outside for the next three hours until my father came at the appointed time to pick me up. But it was drizzling rain and I had no umbrella, so I was forced inside.

Walking into the school that night was worse than walking in on the very first day. At least then I'd had hope that I was embarking on a promising new chapter in my life, that I would make new friends and have new and wonderful experiences. So far none of that had materialized. And I was sorely disappointed. Walking into the dance, my hopes were far less grand. I was prepared to consider the evening a great success if only someone, just one person, actually talked to me.

As I headed toward the gym, I passed groups of kids who were talking and laughing together. I recognized their faces but still didn't know most of their names, especially those of the upperclassmen. No one acknowledged me.

All the doors to the gym were open, and the band was loud enough to be heard from just about anywhere in the school. Sadly, the fact that they were loud was the only thing they had to recommend them. It took me several minutes to recognize that the song they were playing was "Jumpin' Jack Flash." Mick

Jagger himself would have been forced to ask, "What is that noise you're listening to?"

But the scene in the dimly lit gym could not have been more electric if the Rolling Stones had been there. All the Cissys and CiCis and MeMes and Muffs were dancing with the Chips and the Skyes and the Buzzes and Buffs. Those who weren't dancing stood around the perimeter of the gym in small segregated groups, boys to one side, girls to the other.

I forced myself to go inside and slowly made my way along the wall where most of the girls were. I spotted a group of girls I knew from various classes and headed in their direction.

"Hi," I said, smiling as I stepped up to their little circle, hoping to be invited in.

Some of them cast me sidelong, clearly disinterested glances. Some didn't even bother to look at me. The nicer ones in the group muttered a halfhearted "hi." Then they tightened the circle and continued giggling and chatting as if I didn't even exist.

I stood there trying to figure out what to do next, trying not to look as stupid and pathetic and lost as I felt. The lump that was growing in my throat was beginning to choke off my air supply. And I had to bite my lip to keep it from trembling.

I scanned the area for another familiar face. Almost immediately, one appeared. It was a boy from my English class, a cute boy. And he was headed in my direction. And he was smiling.

My chest tightened. I couldn't even try to suck any air in past the lump in my throat. I tried to work the muscles in my face to form a smile, but I couldn't tell if it was working. All I felt were pins and needles. And fear. What would I say to him?

"Hi," I squeaked as he strode up to me, looking so sure of himself.

He strode right past me.

The circle of girls that had closed so tightly to keep me out broke open to envelop him.

"So, who wants to dance?" he said with all the bravado he could muster.

The girls giggled and shot tentative looks at one another.

I do, I thought. But I didn't dare say it, sure that it would elicit riotous laughter from anyone within earshot.

"I'll dance with you." Anne—with an *e*—took up the challenge with even more bravado than that with which it was offered.

And off they went, to the great delight of all her friends.

I felt small and insignificant as I watched them. They were playing a game that I didn't understand. And somehow I felt like the loser. It's easy to feel that way when you're standing alone in a crowded room where everyone else seems to be having a wonderful time.

I had to get out of there. I needed some time alone to figure out what to do. So I headed for the bathroom. But there was no privacy to be found there, just a long line that trailed out the door and halfway down the hallway. But I found that standing quietly in line was preferable to risking any more rejection. After I finished in the first bathroom, I made the rounds of all the others, happy to find a long line in each. I managed to kill close to an hour standing in one line after another, enough time for me to be able to call my father.

"Daddy" was all I managed to get out when he picked up the phone.

"I'm on my way" was all he said.

It was all he had to say. All I wanted to hear. I held back tears of relief as I hung up the phone.

Because I couldn't bear to go back into the dance, I waited for him in front of the school in the drizzling rain, listening to "Jumpin' Jack Flash" blaring inside again. Apparently that was one of the half-dozen songs that the band knew how to play. Well, sort of.

My father was there in no time at all, which was no big surprise really. He usually broke the speed limit backing out of the driveway.

As soon as he pulled the car over to the curb, all the tears I'd been holding back spewed forth. I threw the door open before he'd even come to a complete stop and jumped in.

"Baby! You're soaking wet. And you're crying. What's wrong?" He threw the car into park and turned in his seat to give me his full attention.

"Nothing." I turned my face away in shame. "Let's just go."

"First tell me what's the matter," he insisted.

"No. First get me out of here."

He only hesitated for a moment before he put the car in gear and pulled away from the curb. I put my face in my hands and began to sob. He put his arm around me and pulled me close.

"What happened in there, Chicken?"

"Nothing happened. Not a single, lousy thing."

"Well then why are you crying?"

"I don't know." I sobbed in earnest.

"Did somebody say something to hurt your feelings?"

"No. Nobody even talked to me."

"What do you mean, Baby?"

"Just what I said. Nobody talked to me." I didn't mention that I didn't talk to anybody either. "It was creepy in there, Daddy. You should have seen it. Nobody was acting normal. All the girls stood in little groups, giggling. And all the boys stood around drooling. And I stood there all by myself, like a jerk. And nobody asked me to dance!" I shouted, surprising myself with what I'd said. Then I went back to sobbing.

"My poor baby girl."

"It's because I'm ugly, Daddy."

He laughed and I pulled away from him. "I'm sorry, Baby.

I'm not laughing at you. I'm laughing at the way teenagers are. It's no different from when I was that age. Come on." He pulled me close again. "The boys don't stay away from you because you're too ugly; they stay away because you're too pretty."

"Don't lie. It doesn't help. I'm ugly; big nose, big ears, buck-teeth; and I just have to learn to live with it." It was my own fault. I should have taken him up on his offer of plastic surgery, and then I wouldn't have to go through life looking like Quasimodo's twin sister.

"You're not ugly. Will you listen to me." His voice was reprimanding. "I wouldn't lie to you about this. You're a pretty girl, too pretty for your own good. Or mine. You're the prettiest girl I've ever seen."

"Okay, fine. I know you're not lying. I know you believe that with all your heart. But consider this—a father vulture thinks his kid is the prettiest kid he's ever seen too; so does a father snake. And boys wouldn't ask them to dance either."

"Now listen to me, because you're being silly about this. I'm going to explain to you how boys are. Boys are afraid of pretty girls and even more afraid of smart girls. You see, a girl like that is more likely to say no when you ask her to dance. And boys don't like to get shot down like that. It hurts their egos. They can't stand to have their egos hurt. It's easier to dance with an ugly girl or a dippy girl."

"What about *my* ego?" I was suddenly more angry than hurt.

"Boys don't know you have one. Most girls don't anyway. You didn't cry in there, did you?"

"Of course not!"

"Then your ego should be just fine. You'll see, someday you're going to laugh about tonight. Someday you'll be rich and famous and you'll have men falling all over you. And they'll be great-looking men with lots of money and lots of smarts, not pimply, goofy boys. Then I'm going to remind you of tonight and we'll laugh about this. And you'll know that Daddy's always right about what he tells you. Right?"

I nodded, still crying, still not convinced.

My father sighed heavily. I could tell that he'd run out of sensitivity, that he was racking his brain trying to think of a way to make it all better for me.

"I've got an idea," he said finally. "You wanna drive the car?"

"Really?"

"Yeah, really." He pulled over to the side of the road. Then he opened his door and got out. "Slide over," he told me.

As I got behind the wheel, he went around the back of the car and got in on the passenger's side. "Don't tell your mother," he said as he slid in close and put his arm around me, prepared to grab the steering wheel in an instant if need be. "Promise."

"Of course."

"Okay. Take the steering wheel, left hand at ten o'clock, right hand at two o'clock. Good. Now put your foot on the brake and put the car into gear. Turn the wheel a little to the left so that you can pull out onto the road while you ease down on the gas."

We jerked a little bit, and he helped guide my steering until we were moving along in a straight line at a rip-roaring ten miles an hour.

"Terrific," he said calmly. "You're doing fine."

My heart was pounding with fear and excitement.

"Give it a little more gas," he instructed. "Let's try to get up to at least twenty miles an hour."

The muscle in my calf was already aching from trying to control the amount of pressure I put on the gas pedal. I held on to the wheel as tightly as I could, thanking God that the road was straight and amazed at how much I had to struggle to keep a steady course even on a straight road.

"That's it." My father was encouraging. "You've got it now. Look at that, you're really in control."

He was right. The further I drove away from the dance, the more in control I felt.

While my father's solutions to problems weren't likely to be found on the pages of any parenting manual, they often worked for the sole reason that his heart was in the right place.

≈

Chapter 13

The Mafia Princess

I⸤T WAS⸥ clear to me that I was never going to be accepted into any of the cliques in my new WASPy, preppy high school. Even the geeks didn't want me. Even the geeks were blond-haired and blue-eyed, with hyphenated last names and DAR eligibility if not actual membership. I simply did not blend.

But there was an upside to it. If no one bothers to talk to you, there are no distractions to keep you from your schoolwork. If no one will deign to eat lunch with you or even allow you to sit at their table, you can take your brown bag with your greasy salami sandwich into an empty classroom and finish off your homework so that you never have to carry a book to and from school.

Hey, "you gotta do whatcha gotta do." From great emperors to common street thugs, those were the words of wisdom that were passed down to me from generation to generation. Words to live by. I did my best.

So here's what I had to do. First and foremost, I had to put forth the image that everything was perfect. My parents worked hard to give me every opportunity—opportunity for what, I wasn't quite sure. But I got the message loud and clear that everything they did, they did for me; and in return, it was my responsibility not to let them down. That meant I had to bring home straight A's. Anything less was bound to elicit a first-degree interrogation by my father to determine exactly how and why I had "fucked up."

I rarely "fucked up." And in the age when "peace, love, and water beds" ruled supreme, I never, ever got "fucked up," mostly because I was never invited to any parties. But I did spend most of my time walking around feeling perpetually "fucked," though I never did say that word out loud.

Nonetheless, I kept a smile on my face. And every once in a while I even managed to convince myself that I could make things better if only I tried a little harder.

The day that open tryouts were announced for the school play, I decided that it was time to give myself another push. After all, I put on an Oscar-award-winning performance every day of my life; I figured I might as well put that talent to some practical use.

The play was *The Prime of Miss Jean Brodie*. I immediately bought a copy from the school store and began to study it diligently. I never, for a moment, allowed myself to believe that I might actually land the title role. That role would almost certainly be given to a senior. Rightfully so. And I had no doubt that she would also be a blond. I was correct on both counts.

The role I pursued, the one I desperately wanted because I was sure it fit me like a glove, was the part of Sandy, the troubled misfit.

My audition went brilliantly. If I'd had to choose one word to describe my interaction with everyone in the theater that day, "misfit" would definitely have been at the top of the list. While everyone else arrived in little groups, or at least in pairs, I walked in all by myself.

As I stood at the back of the theater, looking down at the stage where the others were lined up to sign in, I considered my options. I could turn tail and run. I could hurl myself down the stairs and put an end to my miseries once and for all. Or I could get in line, add my name to the list, and wait my turn to show them all just how dramatic I could be.

My father always told me, "You'll never get anywhere in this life, Baby, without a set of balls." I knew he was right. So the choice was obvious. I reached deep down, rearranged my metaphorical balls, and prepared to step up to the plate.

While the wait seemed like an eternity, my turn at bat came and went in a blur. "That was very nice. Thank you," the teacher/director said after we'd exchanged our few lines of dialogue. Had he even noticed that I wasn't reading from the book, that I'd done the scene from memory? Did he think that I had done a good job? Had I? He wasn't giving anything away. It was nothing personal. The perfunctory tone in his voice wasn't reserved just for me. He was an equal opportunity ego destroyer. But I didn't have a cheering section in the audience to look to for a wink, a nod of approval, or a thumbs-up. The best that I could do was make a graceful exit.

I was surprised to find that I left the building that day feeling quite pleased with myself. First of all, the little voice inside me, the one that never lies, told me that I had done a good job.

Secondly, I couldn't help but admire my own *coglioni*; I had the balls to keep on trying in the face of nothing but rejection. And lastly, my departure this time hadn't reduced me to tears.

I was even more surprised to find that my name was on the callback list the next morning.

Two days later, I read again for the part of Sandy. In the smaller, more competitive group, where camaraderie had degenerated into every-man-for-himself, my confidence soared. My reading of the part I wanted was exemplary; so good, in fact, that I was asked to stay and repeat it not once, but twice. I was sure I had it in the bag. But what really thrilled me was the thought of becoming involved in something, that I might finally find a place where I could feel a sense of belonging.

Most surprising of all, I got the part of Sandy.

Well, sort of.

There are actually two Sandys in the play—the young Sandy, who is the troubled teenager, and the adult Sandy, who has turned her back on her troubled past by becoming a nun.

Sandy, the nun, is a character in the play too.

Well, sort of.

She's more of a ghost really, the narrator who sets the stage without ever interacting with any of the other characters.

That was the part I was given. It certainly put the exclamation point on the fact that I was the only Italian Catholic girl in the school.

So much for belonging.

Except for dress rehearsal, I didn't even practice with the rest of the cast. So even when I was allowed to join, I was still the odd man out. But once again, I found my *coglioni* and made the best of it.

My parents were so thrilled that I had gotten a part in the play that they were prepared to buy every seat in the theater for opening night. My father could have easily done it from the cash in his pocket and still have had enough left over to buy himself a new Cadillac. But thankfully, all students, even cast members, were limited to six tickets per show, and even that was on a first-come-first-serve basis.

I got my six tickets—per show. And on opening night, and every subsequent night thereafter, my mother, my father, my uncle, my aunt, and my two sisters were there, front and center.

Much as I hated the part that I was forced to play, I gave it my all, not only for my personal cheering section but also for myself.

I did a good job. The applause I got when I took my bows came not only from the sound of twelve hands clapping, but also from the entire audience. And I received flattering reviews in the school and local newspapers.

But, in the end, it was my father and my uncle who really stole the show. In a school auditorium where other fathers' ties served as little billboards for Ivy League mascots, my father's and uncle's Italian silk ties advertised nothing but danger. Whereas other dads were bespectacled in nerdy horn-rimmed glasses, my dad wore dark glasses, even in a dark auditorium, even at night. Yes, it made him look shady. And it made him look tough. But that wasn't why he wore them. He wore dark glasses because he'd had an accident when he was a child that left him blind in one eye. It also left him with no muscle control over that eye. The eye wandered. It was rarely in line with where his good eye was focused. He was terribly self-conscious about it. So he covered it as best he could.

Uncle Gene wore dark glasses because he thought his older brother looked cool and he wanted to be cool too. Or maybe he just wanted my father to think that everything was cool.

In any case, the glasses were another sign of trouble. So were the custom-made suits. And the Italian leather shoes.

The rumors spread like wildfire until the whispers behind

my back became deafening. I pretended to be oblivious. That was the wrong choice. Of course, there was no right choice. People are determined to believe what they want to believe. Things would have been far worse had I protested too much. That was why I'd opted for silence, which is almost always the lesser of two evils. When in doubt, take the Fifth.

My schoolmates were more frustrated than every DA in America. On the last night of the play, one of them finally snapped. We were out onstage taking our final bow to a roaring, standing ovation. The girl next to me had played one of the young Sandy's school chums. She had never uttered a single word to me before. But that night when we joined hands, as we were forced to do, she tugged hard to get my attention. As I turned toward her, she leaned in and shouted into my ear, "So is your father in the Mafia or what?"

Her voice was so loud, I was sure that everyone in the audience had heard what she said. My eyes went immediately to my family. But they were all smiles and applause. Uncle Gene put two fingers in his mouth and whistled. I smiled at him, then scanned the crowd. Other whistles went up, cheers, more applause. The audience was too boisterous to have heard anything.

She tugged on my hand again. "Well?" she demanded, shamelessly.

Of course she was shameless. She was in her element, surrounded by her friends and family, on her own social turf. I was the outcast; and my poor, unsuspecting family was the subject of ridicule. She stood there smirking at me, waiting for me to burst into tears.

I did want to cry. But that was not an option. So instead, I launched into the best performance I would ever give on that stage. I laughed as if she'd just told me the best joke ever. To the audience, it might have appeared that we were great friends, except that she wasn't smiling anymore. "You must be kidding," I said. "Don't you read the papers?" Then I leaned in close so that no one else could hear me or read my lips. "Everybody knows that there is no such thing as the Mafia."

As I leaned back, I squeezed her hand hard so that she was forced to look at me. I winked at her and laughed again.

Before I even left the stage, I had begun to prepare myself for a new role.

Yes, Virginia, There Is a Mafia

WITH THE *Godfather* at the top of the best-seller list, all of America was pretty convinced that the Mafia was a reality. And everybody in my school was completely convinced that my father was a very important player. Since there was nothing I could do to divest them of this misconception, I decided that I might as well use it to my best advantage whenever possible.

Suddenly, my schoolmates were actually talking to me. "I saw you in the play," they would say. "You were really good."

"Thanks," I'd say, demurring to the overly enthusiastic compliment. "That's nice of you to say." I knew that what they were thinking and what they really wanted to say was, "I saw your father at the play. He's pretty scary-looking. Is he really in the Mafia?" I knew this because I'd heard them say it to one another.

The answer was that he wasn't. But he was a criminal defense attorney. And he did have some very colorful clients whose "alleged" exploits were often covered in local newspapers.

Just a few days after the play, in fact, my father had to deliver his most notorious client to the state prison. They were photographed outside the prison gates. And the picture appeared on the front page of the paper.

The reason for the incarceration of this gentleman—and he was a gentleman, despite all allegations to the contrary—was hardly front-page news. This particular "alleged" Mafia don was being sent to jail for "contempt of court."

It had become a favorite tactic of prosecutors who wanted to "break the back of the Mafia" to grant immunity to certain key players in return for their testimony against others. Refusing to testify resulted in being charged with contempt of court and being sent to jail.

Violating *omertà*—the vow of silence—resulted in a bullet to the brain, or worse.

Needless to say, nobody talked. And a lot of wise guys went to jail for contempt of court, every single one of them disavowing any knowledge of the existence of an organization called the Mafia. And despite the fact that most of them did speak Italian, they all appeared to be equally puzzled by any reference to La Cosa Nostra.

This "imaginary" organization without a single member of record became an endless source of fascination. Anybody who knew somebody who knew somebody became something of a celebrity and was likely to be quoted in the papers.

I knew somebody who knew somebody. And both of them had said "no comment" to the newspapers.

There is nothing in the world guaranteed to whet the appetite for gossip more than an official "no comment."

The day my father had "no comment" for the newspapers, everybody in school wanted to talk to me. I did not eat my lunch alone in an empty classroom. Instead, I found myself holding court at a packed table in the cafeteria. Ironically, the lunch special that day was "English muffin pizzas."

Fortunately, a toasted English muffin with a squirt of ketchup and some Cheez Whiz on top has no real smell to it. But the very sight of such a thing had me gagging on my beautiful roast pork sandwich. No matter, since I didn't really have time to eat anyway.

"So do you know this guy?" The question came from at least three people at once. All eyes were on me. It felt good to be the center of attention, even if it was for all the wrong reasons.

"I've met him," I answered coyly, telling the truth, the whole truth, and nothing but the truth. I had met him. One night he came into the restaurant where my father had taken us out to dinner. He came over to our table. Introductions were made. I politely said hello, received a warm smile, a pat on the cheek, a compliment for my ladylike demeanor; and that was that. To me, he was just a cute little old Italian guy, like so many others I'd met along the way. Well, except for the rumors.

"I heard he was a triggerman on the Albert Anastasia hit in New York during the big Mafia wars back in the fifties," one of the jocks tossed out enthusiastically.

"Yeah," another joined in. "I heard that was how he made his bones."

"Triggerman?" "Made his bones?" Where were these guys getting this stuff?

"Oh my God," the dippy, blond cheerleader at the end of the table shrieked. "Check out page thirty-two at the bottom." She passed around her copy of *The Godfather* for inspection.

The scene that had so scandalized her was the one in which Sonny Corleone snuck away from his sister's wedding with one of her bridesmaids for a "quickie" inside the house.

"Does that stuff really happen?" she asked me, as if I were an expert on Mafia sex habits. I hadn't even had my first date.

I rolled my eyes and shook my head, thinking, *You've got to be kidding me.*

But everyone else at the table read my reaction as, *You've got to be kidding me, it happens all the time in my house.*

"Cool," one of the preppie dorks proclaimed.

"Yeah, very cool," another agreed.

"So what about the other stuff." The jock who was sitting next to me returned to the main topic of conversation. "Did this guy really do that hit in New York, or what?"

I wondered how I should answer. I had no firsthand knowledge. But neither did the feds. And still the story kept circulating. It was what I'd heard. When I'd asked my father, my uncle, or any of their friends about it, the answer I got was always, "That's what I heard." I'd even heard that the don himself, when asked about it, is alleged to have answered, "That's what I heard."

"That's what I heard," I parroted the non-answer. Of course, coming from someone with dark hair, dark eyes, olive skin, and a last name that ended in a vowel, that was tantamount to a full confession straight from the horse's mouth.

"And you know this guy," the jock said with a tone of reverence in his voice.

I shrugged, standing behind my first answer; I had met him. I knew full well that my shrug was, in effect, a "no comment." And I took great pleasure watching them all as their imaginations worked furiously to color in all the blank spaces that I'd left for them.

The truth was that I was every bit as intrigued by the Mafia as they were, and every bit as removed from it. My father did not bring these guys home for dinner. All he ever brought home really were some amusing anecdotes. And a lot of money. In fact, the ways in which he sometimes got paid for his services were the most amusing stories of all, ones that we were never allowed to tell. We got a pool table once. And a pinball machine. And a freezer full of meat—steaks and roasts and chops and fillets, delivered inside a big, shiny, new freezer. He was once paid with a bag of gold coins. And another time with a bag full of silver dollars. Sometimes he'd bring home jewelry or antiques. But my sisters and I always liked it best when he got paid in cold, hard cash, with bills of small denominations.

Whenever my father had a whole lot of small bills, we'd talk him into playing our favorite family game, Money to the Peasants. My sisters and I would gather in the foyer while my father went up the stairs to the balcony overhead. Then he would begin tossing paper money into the air until everything he had in his bag was gone. Whatever we managed to catch before it touched the floor was ours to keep. It's a lot more difficult than it sounds. And we rarely pocketed more than twenty dollars apiece. But with real money in the offing, it was a good deal more fun than a game of Monopoly.

These were tales I'd never tell in school. Our private life

was private. Besides, the details of my day-to-day existence were of no real interest to the progeny of the horse thieves who'd colonized these United States. What they wanted to hear were stories of the newer, more glamorous outlaws.

I did have stories. And those stories were the currency I used to buy my way into "polite society."

My father told me it was okay for me to repeat what he had said to the "alleged" don as he turned him over to the prison warden. It was a great joke after all, worth repeating. The don himself had laughed out loud. So had the warden. "Whatever you do," my father had said as he shook his hand in farewell, "please don't kiss me." He was referring, of course, to the infamous "kiss of death" that was supposed to have preceded a Mafia hit.

My father got a hearty handshake, a pat on the back, but no kiss. Still, he was a little jittery. And a few weeks later he was completely convinced that we were all marked for death. This time it was my mother's fault.

My father was working late at the office on yet another case involving a pair of colorful characters who'd been charged with racketeering—booking numbers to be specific. A call came to our private, unlisted phone number from the state prison. My mother politely informed the client that my father was not home. She took his "urgent" message and assured him that she would relay it to my father as soon as she spoke to him. An hour later, a second call came. My mother repeated what she had said the first time, going on to explain that my father was working late and that he was incommunicado, even to her, but that as soon as she spoke to him, she would pass on the message. An hour later the phone rang again. Again my mother was polite.

But when the call came at midnight, waking her from a

sound sleep, her patience disintegrated. "I told you I would give him your message," she growled into the receiver. "And I will. There is nothing else I can do for you. So please stop calling here."

"Do you know who I am?" the voice from the state pen asked.

"I don't care who you are," my mother told him. "I have three children who have to go to school in the morning. And right now, who you are, is the person who is keeping us all from having a good night's sleep." She hung up the phone.

The next morning, she related the story to my father, emphasizing her exasperation with this criminally insensitive human being who, in her opinion, deserved to be locked up on that basis alone.

I watched in fascination as my father turned white—whiter than any of my near-albino, WASPy schoolmates. Beads of sweat appeared on his upper lip. And the muscles in his jaw began to twitch. This was big trouble. "Do you know what you've done?" he said to my mother, his voice barely above a whisper. "You've killed us all."

My mother rolled her eyes at him, completely unmoved by the melodrama.

"Do you know who this guy is?" my father squeaked, barely able to force out any sound.

"Yeah, yeah, yeah." My mother waved him off, unimpressed. "He explained it all to me. I've read the papers. I know who he is. But that doesn't give him the right to call here at all hours of the night and wake me up and wake up the kids when I already explained to him that you weren't home."

"We're dead," my father announced as he left the room.

"Just ignore him," my mother told us once he was out of earshot. "Your father's nuts." This was not news to us. We'd heard it before. And we knew she was right. So none of us worried.

Nobody put out a contract on any of our lives. The results, in fact, were quite the opposite. From that point on, my mother was treated with all the respect that was due only to a "made member." Word spread quickly that this was a broad that had real *coglioni*. We began to get special treatment at pizza parlors, Italian delis, bakeries, and restaurants—extra toppings on the pizza, a nice salami, a few more cannoli or *sfogliatelle,* a bottle of wine on the house.

But my father still had to work for his living. Good thing too. Because it was his name in the papers that provided me with the only attention I ever got from my peers at school. They never tired of hearing about the exploits of the people in the "underworld."

So I told them about the pair of bookies my father defended. They were both "made guys." And if it hadn't been for my father, they would both have been in jail. The cops had them dead-to-rights. Two police officers had walked into their "club" while these guys were on the phone taking bets. Two police officers with exemplary records of service had testified to the fact that they had seen the slips of paper on which all these illegal bets had been recorded. Unfortunately, the police officers were not able to confiscate said receipts because they were all written on "flash paper."

Both officers went on to explain that "flash paper" was something that was often used by professional bookies. It was paper that was treated with chemicals that made it highly flammable. All you had to do was touch a match to "flash paper" and it virtually exploded in a burst of flame, leaving no ash and no evidence. My father's clients were pros. Their "flash paper" was gone before the cops came through the door.

The prosecutor had no tangible evidence. His entire case was built on the word of the two cops. But that was enough, because the jury believed them.

My father and his clients were in a real bind. And they all knew it.

The clients came up with an answer. They would find a way to "get rid of" the judge.

My father explained to these two wise guys that if some unfortunate mishap were to befall the judge during their trial, suspicion would naturally fall on them. He made it quite clear that if such a thing were to occur, they would be forced to hire new counsel.

The clients promised to behave—as long as my father promised to get them acquitted. The pressure was on. For the next few weeks, my father rarely slept. He worked the problem day and night until he finally found the answer.

"Flash paper." It was just regular paper that was treated with chemicals. The trick to "flash paper" was that you couldn't handle it too much. The more it was handled, the more the chemicals wore off, making it just regular paper again—paper that burned slowly and left a residue.

Like P. T. Barnum, my father went into court and put on a great dog and pony show. He produced, for the inspection of everyone present, a piece of genuine "flash paper." He asked several experts, including the arresting officers, to testify to its authenticity. He made sure that everyone had a good look at this magical "flash paper"; the judge, the witnesses, the jury, and anyone else he could get to touch it. And when he was sure that all traces of the chemicals had been worn off, he asked the officer on the witness stand, "So, if I were to set this piece of paper on fire, it would go up in a quick spark, leaving nothing behind?"

"That is correct," the officer testified under oath.

"Nothing at all," my father clarified. "Not even a bit of ash."

"That's right," the officer reiterated unflinchingly, secure in his convictions. He knew what he knew. And what he knew was correct. Unfortunately, he didn't know what my father knew.

Even the defendants didn't know what my father knew.

So when my father struck a match and touched it to the infamous "flash paper," no one in that courtroom dared draw a breath.

The corner of the paper picked up the flame and my father held on brazenly as the paper curled and burned and dropped ash onto his shoes. He only blew it out when the flame began to lick his fingertips. He said nothing at all. He didn't have to. His little demonstration negated the testimony of both policemen. His clients were acquitted. The judge was safe. And that night, we played Money to the Peasants.

The "flash paper" story was a crowd pleaser.

The story of the "Mafioso" who had invented a machine that could grind the human body up into the size of a meatball was another winner.

And the information about the body that was found in the trunk of an abandoned car in the airport parking lot, the day before the newspapers reported the story, guaranteed my celebrity status.

I was the Scheherazade of the lunchroom. As long as I had scoop, I was worth something. Even upperclassmen began to smile at me in the hallways and say "hello." Some even stopped to chat.

Still I knew that I was nothing more than a curiosity. While I may have been amusing, I certainly wasn't one of them. To tolerate my presence on school grounds was one thing, to bring me into their homes was quite another. It was simply out of the question. So while I had found a way to break out of solitary confinement and mingle with the general population during school hours, it did nothing to improve my social life. I still never got asked for a date, or invited to any party.

≈

Chapter 15

Enter Prince Charming

O N T H E days when I had no stories to tell, or when I didn't have the strength to put on the dog and pony show, I retreated to my empty classroom. There was always homework to be done. And if not that, I always carried a book into which I could disappear.

But one day, my private reverie was interrupted by a boy. A cute boy. The most popular boy in my class.

"Hey," he called to me from the doorway. "What are you doing, sitting in there all by yourself?"

I looked up over the top of my book to see him standing just outside the threshold, as if some invisible barrier prevented him from entering the room. "Just reading," I told him, indicating the book in my hand with a nod. I was rereading *The Great Gatsby,* trying to understand what all the other girls found so romantic about a dark and tragic story of how an outsider tried to win love in the vapid world of the elite.

"How come?" He sounded like the dumb jock I had assumed he was.

"Because I like to read." I tried hard not to sound supercilious. It was something I had a tendency to do. My father found it hateful. First of all, because it was hateful. And secondly, because it was a behavior I'd learned from him.

The cute boy in the doorway chuckled, oblivious to my attitude problem. "I meant, how come you're sitting in there all by yourself and not at lunch with everybody else?" he clarified.

"I guess I just felt like being alone," I answered honestly. And, anxious to get the focus off myself, I turned the tables and asked, "Why aren't you at lunch with everybody else?"

"I had to go to the office," he answered, not explaining any further. "I was headed for the cafeteria when I saw you sitting here looking kind of lonely."

On the surface, it sounded like a cheap come-on. But his tone said something different. Suddenly, I did feel a little bit lonely.

"I'm okay." I shrugged it off. "Just reading." I nodded toward the book again.

"You want some company?" He broke the invisible barrier and strode into the room, not really giving me a choice.

"Sure." I smiled. It wasn't as if I could really throw him out after all. He had as much right to be in that classroom as I did. So I closed my book and put it down on the desk in front of me. I was sitting behind the teacher's desk beside the window.

He took the student's desk directly opposite. "I like the stories you tell," he said as he sat down. "You're very funny, you know."

Not exactly what a girl wants to hear. I wasn't laughing.

"I mean the way you tell stories," he said, tripping all over himself, trying to make it sound like a compliment.

For some reason, I decided to cut him a break. "Well, thanks, I guess."

"No, I mean it." He didn't know when to let it go. "You're funny. You really are."

Funny how? I wanted to ask. But I didn't. I just smiled and nodded noncommittally. He'd sounded so ingenuous after all. Still, I'd had enough experience with my peers there to know not to trust it. As I quickly sized up the situation, I decided that the only reason he'd come in to talk to me was so that he could get an exclusive story that he could retell later to enhance his own popularity. I also decided that he wasn't going to get one.

An awkward silence followed.

He was the one who broke it. "You think most of the kids here are real jerks, don't you?"

If he'd meant to knock me off balance, he almost succeeded. But I'd been trained well enough to know how to hide behind the Fifth Amendment for as long as it took to figure out the other guy's game. I refused to answer on the grounds . . .

"You don't have to say it." He smiled, again seeming oddly ingenuous. "I know what you must think."

"Do you?" I said, allowing a little bit of pomposity to seep out around the edges. The truth was that I was getting a little nervous because I couldn't get a read on this guy's game.

"Yeah, I do," he answered, relaxing back in his seat. He stretched out his legs and crossed them at the ankles and put his hands behind his head. "You want to know why?"

I didn't really. I'd stayed away from the lunchroom specifically to avoid having to play games that day. But since there was no graceful way to escape, I said, "Why?"

I wasn't at all prepared for what he said next. "I feel the same way too."

"Sure you do." I made it clear that I wasn't buying it. And I went on to explain why. "You're the most popular guy in the class."

"Yeah," he admitted without even a hint of false modesty. "I am. But the funny thing about that is I don't feel like I have one real friend."

So the most popular guy in class was every bit as lonely as I was. Imagine that, a teenager with feelings of dejection and isolation and contempt for his peers. But I was touched that he'd admitted it to me. And it was the start of a beautiful friendship.

More often than not, we'd pass the lunch hour in that empty classroom, alone together. We'd talk about our classes, our teachers, our peers. We'd talk about religion, philosophy, and the war in Vietnam. And I'd tell him stories, even the ones I wasn't supposed to repeat.

He thought I was funny. And I loved to make him laugh.

Then one day, he blew the whole thing apart.

"What would you say if I asked you to go out with me?"

Oh no. No, no, no, no, no, no, no. NO. That was a non-question. A setup. A potential lose-lose situation for me. Friend or no friend, I was not about to risk my self-esteem on an honest answer. But I was not about to screw it up beyond repair either. It was, after all, a question I'd been longing to hear, without the "what-would-you-say-if" disclaimer.

While I wasn't exactly country club material, I had learned enough about tennis to know that the most important thing to do was to keep the ball in play. It was up to me to hit it back and keep it in bounds.

"I'd ask you where you were taking me," I shot back.

He laughed. Nervously? "Your father's right about you. You are a wise guy." And then he changed the subject.

Weeks went by without any mention of our uncomfortable little exchange. It was the closest I'd ever come to being asked for a date, and I blew it. I was convinced that I was destined to become a *zitella* just like Aunt Brigit, in a black dress, with a mustache and a goiter and a hunchback.

I began to mope around even more dramatically than the average teenage girl. My mother just ignored me. But my father couldn't bear up under the pressure. "What's the matter, Chicken?" he asked, over and over.

Once we'd established the fact that it wasn't just "female problems," he demanded an answer.

So I explained what had happened.

And my father laughed.

"It's not funny," I told him.

"Yeah, it is," he said. "You want to know why?"

I didn't really. But there was no point in saying that to him. Once my father decided that he had to explain something to somebody, he could pontificate for hours. Any protests only prolonged the agony. So I listened quietly as he told me once again about boys and their fragile egos. It was clearly a subject that was near and dear to his heart. He wrapped it all up by telling me, "By being a wise guy, you scared the poor kid away."

"So now what am I supposed to do?" I wanted to know. And something told me I should have been asking my mother.

"You've got to find a way to build up his ego and let him know that you're interested in him too," he said. "Without acting like a 'chewn-gum,' " he added as a caveat.

"Chewn-gum." I never knew where he got that word. I was pretty sure he'd made it up himself. He used it to refer to the stereotypical loudmouthed, big-haired girl who always had a cigarette in her hand, a wad of gum in her mouth, and not much else in her head. For him, it was also a euphemism for "slut." He'd always made it clear to me, in no uncertain terms, that he would "drown me in the pool" before he would allow me to become such a creature. Compared to the big-haired girls, Medusa, with her head full of snakes, was a raving beauty, at least in my father's estimation.

"I am not now, nor will I ever be, a 'chewn-gum,' " I assured him with no small degree of indignation. It was true. I simply did not have it in me to act like the kind of girl that men seemed to adore. But secretly I wished that if there were such a thing as reincarnation, in my next go-around, I would come back as a dumb blond. I really did need to have more fun.

"Just remember," my father told me, "you're the one who calls all the shots."

I talked to my mother about it. And she said pretty much the same thing. It was so rare for my mother to concede that my father had made sense about anything, that I took their advice as seriously as if I'd heard it from a burning bush.

Now all I had to do was figure out how to get the doofus that I'd grown to like so much to try to ask me for a date again.

There was no way to be cool about it. One day, when we were sitting there alone in our classroom, I blurted out, "Do you remember when you asked me what I would say if you asked me to go out with you?"

"Yeah." He winced as if I were about to hit him.

I would have liked to, just for his being so dense. But I didn't. Instead, I decided to make it easy for him. "Well, what would you say if I said yes?"

It took a minute for that to register. And just as I was beginning to rethink the offer, he said, "Really?"

Oh, yeah, everything my father had told me about boys was true. But at least this one was better than most. "Yeah," I told him.

"You want to go out with me?" The most popular boy in the class seemed shocked that the pariah really liked him.

"Yeah," I answered.

"Friday? After school?"

I was nodding in agreement.

"It'll be great," he promised.

I should have asked him where he was taking me.

≈

Chapter 16

You Are What You Eat

D INNER AND a movie. That was the plan for our very first date. It was frighteningly unoriginal. It didn't even reach the heights of being a cliché it was so mundane.

But it was a DATE.

This was serious business. It was so serious, in fact, that my mother felt the need to impart some unsolicited advice.

"About dinner," she said, "just remember that it is not your father who is picking up the bill. Do not order two lobsters." She was referring to the eating competitions that my father and I often engaged in at restaurants. We'd start with an order of clams casino, have two lobsters stuffed with crabmeat as an entrée, and finish off with another order of clams casino for dessert. It was always a draw, since neither of us ever left food on our plates. And my father never flinched when he saw the check. He'd just peel bills off his wad of cash and toss them onto the table.

"Do not even order one lobster," my mother went on. "And don't order clams casino either."

Dating was beginning to sound pretty crummy to me. "What am I supposed to do, eat the bread and drink the water?"

"You're supposed to act polite," she said. "You don't want to bankrupt this kid on the first date, do you?"

"Why can't I just pay for my own?" I asked. "Then I can have whatever I want."

"Because that's not the way it works," she explained. "He asked you for a date. He wants to treat you to an evening of fun."

Two lobsters stuffed with crabmeat sandwiched between two orders of clams casino was always a whole lot of fun for me. But I was not about to argue the point with my mother. When it came to decorum after all, she was the expert. "So what am I allowed to eat?" I asked again.

"The best thing to do is find out what he is going to have, and then you order something less expensive," she advised.

It did seem the polite thing to do. Besides, I could always eat again after I got home. And food wasn't really the point.

Good thing too.

In his attempt to make me feel relaxed and comfortable, my WASPy, preppie, jock date took me to the one and only Italian restaurant in his little Ivy League town. The closest it actually came to being Italian was that the name of the place did end in a vowel. And the red-and-white-checkered tablecloths added a little romance to the *Lady and the Tramp* ambiance.

Going right along with the mood, I ordered the spaghetti and meatballs. It was the cheapest thing on the menu. And since nothing else looked or smelled even remotely appetizing—there wasn't even a hint of garlic in the air—I figured, "What the hell." And I reminded myself that this wasn't about the food.

Good thing too.

The meatballs looked like anemic, little White Castle burgers floating in a puddle of ketchupy goo atop a lump of pasty noodles.

"Looks good," my date said enthusiastically, picking up his knife and fork, ready to dig in.

This boy had a lot to learn.

"Don't cut it," I practically shrieked. I was prepared to put up with a lot for the sake of romance. But I refused to share a dinner table with someone who would cut spaghetti—or in this case, the spaghettilike substance that had been laid before us.

Cutting spaghetti is a sacrilege. The only thing worse than cutting spaghetti is calling it "spaghettis." That, I think, is a capital crime. The word *spaghetti* is already plural. And, no, I don't think there is a singular form. Nobody can eat just one.

If my mother was an authority on dating etiquette, I certainly qualified as an authority on spaghetti etiquette. I wasn't even potty trained before I knew how to twirl spaghetti properly on a fork.

This is the way it is done. You use the tines of your fork to tease out a few strands. Then, touching the tines of the fork to the side of the bowl, or the edge of the plate, you twirl the fork until the spaghetti is wrapped around it in a nice little bite-size ball with no loose ends.

The use of a spoon in this process was strictly forbidden in my house. My grandfather said that only Sicilians ate spaghetti that way. I wasn't sure what that meant, but I knew it wasn't good.

There was only one thing worse than using a spoon.

"Put down the knife," I told my date. "I'm going to teach you how to eat spaghetti."

It wasn't easy, but by the end of the meal, I had him twirling spaghetti on his fork as well as any five-year-old Neapolitan kid could do it. Unfortunately, when he was through, there was almost as much sauce on his shirt as there was in his stomach. But that didn't matter to me.

My father, on the other hand, was horrified.

During the debriefing session that followed the date, my father looked as if he were constantly on the verge of tears. And I didn't even tell him about the good night kiss. Not that there was a lot to tell. It was so innocent that the spaghetti kiss in *Lady and the Tramp* would have been X-rated in comparison. But I knew my father would never understand that.

He didn't understand any of it.

"You like this boy?" The sense of amazement in his voice was a cue to me that I should say no.

"Yes, I do," I said, defying my father. "I like him a lot."

"Why?"

"I don't know. I just do."

My father just stared at me, waiting for a better answer. With my father there always had to be a reason—a good reason, not for his behavior, but certainly for everybody else's.

"Okay," I conceded. "I like him because he's nice. And he's cute. And he's funny. And because he likes me."

"So the kid's got good taste," my father said, latching onto what he perceived to be a positive attribute. "He can't be a total moron. But still, before I let you go out with him again, there are a few things he's going to have to learn. Tell him we're all going out to dinner next Saturday night."

I had the terrible feeling that I was going to end up just like Aunt Brigit. And when my mustache came in and I'd perfected my *strega* powers, I knew exactly who was going to be the recipient of my very first curse.

Still, I'd explained enough about my father on our first date that when I "invited" my new boyfriend out to dinner with the family, he accepted with a surprising sense of good humor, and a not-so-surprising sense of abject terror. Both feelings were justified.

When he arrived at our house at the appointed hour, he was relieved to find that it was not my father who greeted him at the door. I was the one who let him in. We even enjoyed a few moments alone before I led him into the family room to introduce him to my mother and my sisters. My mother welcomed him with open arms, as she did every person who came into her home—and it was her home. My father may have been the one who paid all the bills, but there was no mistaking the fact that he only lived there at her pleasure. Or if not her pleasure, at least at her great forbearance.

There was always plenty of time for my mother to put new guests at ease because my father never failed to be half-past fashionably late. The four females in the house were always dressed and ready to go while he was still preening in front of the mirror. The only thing that took longer than combing his hair to perfection was the arduous task of tie selection.

This was no easy business, since two walls of my father's walk-in closet were lined with tie racks. Every tie he'd ever purchased in his entire life was draped neatly over its own peg along those walls in a great panoply of color and pattern. Some of them were frighteningly outdated, but he refused to part with a single one. No matter how much money he had in his pocket, he could not overcome the poverty mentality that kept him from getting rid of anything that might someday prove useful.

"How's this tie with this suit?" he said to my mother as he stepped into the room. It was his standard entrance line.

The tie he'd chosen for the evening had a black-and-gray background, overlaid with a geometric pattern in white, outlined in gold thread—twenty-four-karat gold thread. Once we'd all assured him that his choice was, as usual, perfect, he turned his attention to my date. "Nice to meet you," he said, shaking hands. "Glad you could join us tonight."

"Thank you for inviting me," my date said politely but about an octave higher than I was used to hearing him speak.

My father winced at the sound, shot a disapproving look at me, but said, "No problem." He let it hang in the air, clearly enjoying the awkward moment of silence, then he said, "Let's go" and headed for the door.

We all piled into the Cadillac, three in front, three in back. My baby sister sat between me and my date, the middle sister sat between my parents, where she most liked to be.

The twenty-minute drive was mercifully quiet, except for Frank Sinatra, Dean Martin, Jerry Vale, and all the others whose songs played constantly on the ginker radio station my father liked.

When we arrived at our destination, I smiled reassuringly at my date, knowing that the only time he'd ever seen anything like it was in the movies, or maybe on the front page of the newspapers when they were covering some big underworld raid.

Even to me, my father's favorite restaurant was a rather unusual place. It reminded me of pictures I'd seen of the "Apalachin Conference," the ill-fated Mafia convention that took place in the late fifties in a big house in upstate New York where the FBI arrested fifty-some Mafia bosses. I never had any trouble at all imagining wise guys jumping out the windows of our little restaurant, trying to escape as the state police surrounded the place. In fact, I often hoped that something like that would happen. But not that night.

That night, as we drove through the open wrought iron gates toward the big old farmhouse, all I wanted was for everything to be normal, or at least as normal as things ever got in my world. To me, that meant no screaming or yelling, no breaking things, and no guns. It wasn't much to ask for, but there was never any guarantee.

My father parked the car next to all the other Cadillacs and Lincolns that were scattered willy-nilly on the lawn in front of the building. There was no parking lot. Nor was there any sign or other discernable feature to distinguish the place as a restaurant. Only the fabulous smells emanating from the kitchen gave it away.

My father herded us all inside. My mother took the lead. He pulled up the rear.

As we entered we were greeted by waiters and patrons alike as members of the family who had just arrived home for dinner. We were gestured toward a big old wooden table covered by a sturdy, and immaculately clean, white cloth, surrounded by serviceable old wooden chairs. No flowers. No candles. No room for such nonsense once the table was laden with food.

I could see the culture shock on the face of the boy from the other side of the tracks. But I could also see a sense of awe and excitement. It was as if he'd stepped into a whole new world. And he had. We might just as well have been in a farmhouse in the countryside somewhere in Italy. Our surroundings were just as plain, and just as beautiful.

Once we'd all settled in, our waiter, who was about my father's age and dressed every bit as well because he was actually one of the owners of the restaurant, came over to take our order.

"You want the baccala salad?" It wasn't really a question.

So my father didn't bother to answer. A shrug and a smile said *of course.*

"Baccala salad for the table," he hollered into the kitchen. He also wrote it down on a little pad, not a receipt book like in other restaurants, just a pad of plain white paper.

My mouth had already begun to water. Baccala salad was another one of those great peasant dishes that I absolutely adored. But then, I was a kid who did my teething on a hard piece of pecorino Romano cheese, so I have always been aware of the fact that my personal tastes are not necessarily shared by the general public. Still, I am of the opinion that a good recipe for baccala salad is worth its weight in gold.

Baccala Salad

Step 1: Check your supply of Chianti. When you're sure you've got plenty on hand, take a trip to the fish market. Pick out a nice piece of baccala, which is dried, salted cod.

Step 2: When you get your fish home, start in on the Chianti while you soak the fish in a big pot of fresh water in the refrigerator for twenty-four hours. Change the water at least four times during this period. Refill your wineglass at your own discretion.

Step 3: When at least twenty-four hours have passed, bring a large pot of water to a full boil. Add the juice of one lemon. Boil the baccala for fifteen minutes. Then drain and cool the fish.

Step 4: Break up the baccala into bite-size pieces. Toss with hot pepper rings, chopped parsley, white wine vinegar, balsamic vinegar, olive oil, and pepper and marinate over night.

It is a wonderful dish to start a meal, as it really gets the taste buds working.

To follow the baccala salad, my father ordered spaghetti and truffles. Again, the waiter hollered into the kitchen. Again, the dish would be served family style, meaning a great big plate would be delivered to the table and we would all help ourselves. I never had any idea that truffles, which are a rare type of mushroom, were considered a delicacy or that they were frightfully expensive. All I knew was that they were delicious. And I was amused that even my mother enjoyed eating a food that had to be gathered with the help of truffle-sniffing pigs.

But after the spaghetti and truffles, it was every man for himself. This was difficult for a newcomer, as there was no menu and all the waiters got a little testy when they actually had to tell you what was available beside the specials—usually two—which they were all too proud to report.

On the subject of newcomers, they were few and far between. The place was something of a local secret. People were initially introduced as guests of long-standing patrons, and if they behaved properly, they were welcome to return. For walk-in diners, it was always questionable whether or not they would be served. Did they look okay? Was there an available table? Was the waiter who greeted them in a good enough mood to allow a stranger to dine with the rest of us?

One thing was certain: When the check came, they would undoubtedly be paying double whatever my father's bill came to.

It was just the way it was done. A long-standing relationship had its benefits. A cheap meal was one of them.

But far and away the best perk was being invited to eat in the kitchen. While being anywhere near the kitchen might seem like something of an insult in the circles of the rich and famous, in my world there were few honors higher than that.

Unless we had company, my mother insisted that we get the one and only table in the kitchen. She liked to watch the cooks so that she could go home and try to re-create their recipes. Sometimes she even got up to help them. And we always got tastes of everything before it was served up for the people in the general dining room.

"Do you want to share the steak for two?" I asked my date, trying to make it as easy as possible for him, and also because it was the best steak anywhere, ever.

"Sure," he agreed quickly, and gratefully. "That sounds good." It was also the first thing that he'd heard ordered that was recognizable to him.

My mother ordered the roast chicken for herself and for my sisters. The chicken was roasted all day with about a bushelful of garlic; it was also the best anywhere, ever. And my father opted for one of the specials, the saltimbocca. Vegetables came "family style."

The food started coming almost immediately, which meant that my father had neither the time nor the inclination to talk— at least not about anything but the food. There was nothing like a good meal to put my father in a state of euphoria. A couple of bites of spaghetti and truffles, and he was everybody's best friend.

It was one long evening of companionable moaning and groaning, first over the pleasure of a feast fit for kings, and deteriorating into the sweet agony of overstuffed stomachs.

My second date was a success. A third, a fourth, and a

fifth followed. And pretty soon his parents were complaining that he was spending more time at my house than he was at his own.

I had a boyfriend.

Still, I was never really sure whether it was me or the food that kept him coming back.

≈

Back to the
Old Country

HAVING A boyfriend, even a popular one, did not make my life at school any easier. In fact, in some ways, it made it more difficult. The girls just scorned me more for having stolen a perfectly good catch. And the boys kept an even greater distance once it was clear that I was "taken," not that any of them ever wanted me in the first place.

Since there was little else for me to do but study, I did get the good education for which my father paid an exorbitantly high tuition. Still, my high school years were a perfect example of caveat emptor, "buyer beware." I knew that my father did not get what he intended to buy. On graduation day, I walked out of that place every bit as much an "outsider" as I was on the first day I walked in. For four years, I was treated like a "big-haired girl." And nothing I ever did could change that. While my father sent me there so that I could have every advantage, I left that place feeling "less than." But I did my best to keep that from him.

On the surface, my father had accomplished what he was so sure his father had wanted for all of us. He was living the American Dream—a big house out in the 'burbs, kids in private schools, fancy cars, nice clothes, and lots of money to burn. But in my heart, I couldn't help wondering if my life would have been happier if we'd just stayed in our little semidetached house in the city where I'd always felt a sense of belonging.

My father, on the other hand, never looked back. He never waxed nostalgic about life in the old neighborhood, never romanticized about the "good old days when we were poor but happy." My father did not believe that those two states of being could coexist. Despite his swarthy Mediterranean appearance, my father worked hard to be an all-American boy.

But while he did not care to examine his own past, he did become more and more curious about his father's past. And so it was planned that the summer after my freshman year in college, we would make the family pilgrimage to Italy.

My father shipped me off to college convinced that I would come home a doctor. This from a man who fainted at the sight of blood. But somehow, like so many other American dreamers, he equated "doctor" with the brightest and the best. And that was what his kid had to be.

I was only three or four years old when this question had been decided. It was the first time my father asked me what I wanted to be when I grew up. I'd just gotten a silly plastic nurse's kit as a birthday present, and I liked playing with the blood-pressure gizmo, so I told him I wanted to be a nurse.

The reaction I got from him couldn't have been more dramatically negative if I'd said I wanted to be a hooker. "Absolutely not!" he practically roared. "I'm going to send you to the best schools and you're going to go all the way to the top. You will not be a nurse. You will be a doctor."

"Okay, Daddy," I agreed, just to quell the temper tantrum and relieved that he didn't confiscate my nurse's kit.

I suppose he felt that it was a harmless toy because as far as he was concerned, I'd already taken the Hippocratic Oath.

By the time I headed off to college in Boston, I had no intention of being either a nurse or a doctor. I found that I had my father's predisposition for wooziness at the first hint of any bodily malfunction. I was quite unlike my mother, who I was sure could hold your decapitated head firmly atop your shoulders as she drove you to the hospital, where she would personally direct a team of surgeons to properly reattach it. *She* should have been the doctor in the family.

But I was good enough at math and science to fake the premed thing until I figured out what it was I really wanted to do in life and, more importantly, the way I would break that news to my father.

As far as I was concerned, the most important class I took in my first semester of college was Italian 101, a language that was not offered in my preppie high school. Despite the fact that I hadn't spoken it in over a dozen years, not since the day my grandfather died, it all came back quite easily. Even the mistakes I made were not entirely incorrect; they were often lapses into Neapolitan dialect.

Saint Ignatius Loyola, founder of the Jesuits, is purported to have said, "Give me a child until the age of five, and he is mine for life." For nearly the first five years of my life, I belonged to my grandfather. And though my cognitive memories of him are nothing more than faded photographs and snippets of interactions, I know that he is the one who shaped my soul. It is his values that guide me through life and the memory of his love—his love for life and his love for me—that sustains me.

I couldn't wait to go back to the place where he was born, to see what he saw, to try to understand what had shaped him.

We entered Rome like Caesars returning from the conquest of faraway lands. Our chariot was a Mercedes limousine complete with a personal chauffeur/tour guide who would be our constant companion for the two-week duration of our stay in the south. Other guides awaited us in Florence and Venice.

We were waved through customs without having to answer a question or open a bag. Finally, I was in a place where I felt as though I blended. And despite the fact that my father had to struggle with the language and was absolutely hopeless with the currency, math having never been his forte, I could tell that he was relaxed, and happy, and comfortable too.

We were never made to feel as though we were simply "rich American tourists," and we were never treated with the disdain that that being "rich American tourists" often inspires in people of other countries. We were Italian-Americans, and as such, we were treated like prodigal sons.

While our guide, Nello, was clearly well paid—and his wardrobe of Brioni suits attested to the fact that he was well paid by all his clients—his warmth was genuine. He wanted to show us everything. He wanted to teach us all the nuances of his part of the world. And most of all, he wanted to remind us of our own heritage.

I hung on his every word, not only because I so desperately wanted to learn, but also because he was as beautiful a man as I had ever seen in my entire life. He was at least ten years older than my own father and he was married with children, but from the moment he kissed my hand in greeting, I was hopelessly in love. The man oozed sex appeal so relentlessly that even my baby sister, who was only eleven years old, couldn't stop looking at him with goo-goo eyes.

There is something about southern Italian men that makes them irresistible. First of all, they carry themselves like gods. This is because their mothers have worked long and hard to instill in them the belief that they are indeed gods. Italian men are insufferable mama's boys—*mammoni* they are called. And they are pampered beyond all reasonable limits. So, having thus been freed from any practical concerns in life, including, often, the need to be gainfully employed, they can devote every waking moment to perfecting the art of bullshit. Make no mistake, it is an art. And when done properly, women and men alike fall hopelessly under its spell.

In southern Italy, all of life is a game. The monetary system is a perfect example of the mind-set. When we were there, the exchange rate was something like two thousand lire to the dollar. For ten dollars, you got twenty thousand lire. A hundred dollars put you close to a quarter of a million lire. And for a thousand dollars, you were a millionaire twice over. If you looked at it with an Italian sensibility, you could feel larger than life. But if you viewed it with our frugal American values, you would always feel that everything cost too much and that you would never have enough money to get what you wanted or needed.

This culture shock hit my father hard on our very first night in Rome. Nello had suggested that we have dinner at a very chic little restaurant on the Via Veneto not far from the Hotel Excelsior, which was where we were staying. He did not join us, insisting that we should enjoy our first evening alone as a family.

The restaurant was like nothing any of us had ever experienced. It was as if we'd stepped into a scene from *La Dolce Vita*. The place was dripping with excess—marble columns, crystal chandeliers, tables laid with gilt fit for an emperor. And the clientele looked as though they'd spent all day in makeup and wardrobe. We rich American cousins in our best finery were positively shabby in comparison. Still, we were given the best table, compliments of Nello, who it seemed was somehow related to the *padrone*—the proprietor of the establishment.

One lavish course after another was laid before us. There were beautiful vegetables, grilled, marinated, or simply tossed with a little olive oil and vinegar. The artichokes were so tender that you could eat them whole; there were no tough leaves and no "choke." The gnocchi were as light and fluffy as cotton balls. The fish was white and flaky and smelled only of the garlic and spices with which it had been prepared. The fruit was sweet, the cheese pungent. And the wine kept coming.

We sat for hours, as did everyone else at every other table. In an Italian restaurant, the object is not to "turn over the tables" as quickly as possible but to prolong the joy of good food and good company. Every meal is a celebration. It is a time for family, friends, and even pets.

A woman at the next table had a small poodle in her lap. Its jeweled collar was only slightly less ostentatious than the necklace worn by its mistress. Throughout the evening, she petted her little dog, cooed to him, kissed him, and fed him from her plate. No one seemed to notice, except, of course, the American tourists. We were jealous. Life seemed so free and easy there, as if it were meant to be enjoyed rather than just endured.

But nothing comes without a price. And at the end of the evening, dinner checks were proffered.

Our bill came to just over three hundred thousand lire. My father took one look at it and almost passed out. "Well, I hope you all enjoyed dinner tonight," he said to us. "Because after this, our vacation is officially over. We're going to have to go home tomorrow and sell the house just to be able to pay for this meal."

"Give me that," I said, taking the check from his hand. I had figured out right away that I was going to have to be the "money guy" on this trip. I knew we were in trouble when my mother tipped the bellhop, who had carried up ten times his own body weight in luggage, a whopping one thousand lire and my father had chided her for her extravagance. She'd given the poor guy the equivalent of fifty cents. To his credit, the bellhop had accepted it graciously and left. Still, I'm not sure what might have happened to us had I not chased after him with a couple of ten-thousand-lira notes and a sincere apology.

"The bill comes to about a hundred and fifty dollars," I informed my father. "Think you can handle it without selling the house?" Considering the fact that we'd flown over first-class, I was pretty sure that he'd be able to cover dinner.

"How did you get to be such a wise guy?" he said, tossing what looked like oversize Monopoly money onto the table.

"I don't know," I said with a shrug. "But I think I heard somewhere that children learn what they live with."

For a flicker of an instant, I could see the wheels turning as he formulated the diatribe in his head. But it never came to fruition. Instead, my father laughed, intoxicated by the magic of the Roman air, or perhaps by the many pitchers of *vino locale* that we had emptied over the course of the evening's meal.

The expression *joie de vivre* may be French, but it is the Italians who practice that philosophy with utter abandon. "The joy of life" is so inherent in their day-to-day existence that there is no colloquialism to describe the feeling. It is simply *la vita*—life.

Every day in Italy is "anything can happen day." If you're looking for structure or strict adherence to any set of rules, don't go there.

We learned all about the "no rules" rule on day two. What did we want to see first, Nello inquired when he arrived just barely within the hour of the agreed-upon time. It was no problem, of course, since my father still needed about five more minutes to finish getting ready himself.

We decided unanimously that our first stop had to be the Colosseum. This was no surprise to Nello, who had obviously dealt with that request so many times before that he could have driven us there blindfolded. And once we were on our way, it felt as though he was driving blindfolded. You see the "no rules" rule is most applicable in Italy when it comes to traffic.

Miraculously, we made it to the Colosseum without a scratch on the Mercedes or a fractured pedestrian in our wake. But even after we'd exited the automobile, we were still at the mercy of the "no rules" rule.

We couldn't get into the Colosseum.

"Why not?" my father wanted to know. He was a little indignant, since he'd incorporated the currency exchange into his thinking and had decided that he was spending millions of something to have a good time.

Nello explained patiently that the guy who sold the tickets wasn't there yet.

My father looked at his watch. It was well past ten o'clock, the time when all businesses, including national monuments, should be up and running. "When is he supposed to be here?" my father demanded.

Nello shrugged. "When he gets here," he said, as if speaking to an idiot.

"And what time will that be?" my father pressed.

Nello just laughed. "It depends," he said. Then he went on to explain. "Did he have a good night's sleep? Did he wake up on time? Did he have a fight with his wife? Did he get stuck in traffic? He'll be here," Nello assured us, "when he gets here. Let's take a walk while we wait."

We strolled around the outside of the Colosseum as Nello recounted its history for us. He explained how this great amphitheater was built on the site of Nero's lake as an insult to the emperor who was so despised by his people that he was given the choice of either committing suicide or being murdered by his own Praetorian Guard. He told us all about the emperor Vespasian, under whose reign construction was begun but who did not live to see its completion. He gave us the histories of all the other emperors who presided over all the great spectacles that the people of Rome so enjoyed. We heard how the amphitheater was flooded to create a small lake for great naval battles, and how women were never allowed to sit in the first tier of seats because the bloodletting was so considerable that the people sitting in those seats were frequently spattered.

I learned more in the twenty minutes we waited for the ticket seller to show up than I had in any history classes I'd ever suffered through. Nello was both a remarkable historian and a shameless storyteller. He mixed fact with fiction effortlessly and always kept his audience in thrall. By the time we got inside, our imaginations had been excited to the point where we could see the battles, hear the roar of the crowd, and exist for a brief moment in another time and place.

The experience was repeated time and again—in the Roman Forum, Saint Peter's Basilica, the Vatican Museum, the Villa Borghese, Piazza Navona, Piazza Venezia, Piazza di Spagna, Piazza del Popolo, the Baths of Caracalla, the Pantheon, the Catacombs, the Appian Way, side trips to Villa d'Este and Hadrian's Villa, and every other point of interest, including Nello's own apartment house. It was nonstop excitement, nonstop learning, and nonstop wonderment. And, of course, because we were in Italy after all, nonstop eating.

My father practically wept with joy at the presentation of every meal. From neighborhood *trattorie* to five-star restaurants, the food was remarkable. While we Americans are so proud of the fact that our technologies for preserving food allow us to have anything at any time of the year, the Italians will serve only what is in season. And once you have tasted a meal prepared with nothing but the freshest ingredients, anything that's been canned, frozen, freeze-dried, or otherwise packaged simply does not qualify as food anymore.

But the highlight of our trip was when we traveled south of Rome to visit Sorrento, Pompeii, and the place where my grandfather was born, a charming little seaside town called Castellammare di Stabia.

The thing that first struck me about Castellammare di Stabia was how little it must have changed since my grandfather had left. Even two world wars had not managed to alter its character. Little old men in jackets and ties and hats sat on benches along the water's edge gossiping about the day's events or simply watching the boats come and go. Women bargained at the markets for the best prices for fish and produce. Men watched women. And children played freely. It had the air of a carnival. But it was just a day in the life. I wished it had been my life.

And I knew that my father had fallen prey to that same longing. He became teary-eyed when he reminisced about his father. He reminded me of the stories my grandfather told about being a little boy and sitting up in the cliffs that surrounded the bay, looking out over the crystal blue water and dreaming about places far, far away.

In the end, he had traveled far, far away, never to return.

But for me, standing there, looking up into those cliffs and picturing the little boy he must have been, I somehow felt as though I were home again. And I knew that I would spend the rest of my life wondering why he had ever left.

A few days later, we had to leave too. None of us wanted to go.

The night before we left Rome, we had dinner with Nello and his family in a beautiful little restaurant in Trastevere on the other side of the Tiber River. It was a night full of laughter and tears, promises and bullshit.

When all was said and done, he took us to the Fontana di Trevi, the famous Trevi Fountain, one of the world's greatest tourist traps. And we all laughed as we pitched the requisite "three coins" over our shoulders into the fountain to guarantee our return to Rome.

And we all believed in the magic.

❦

That's *Amore*

W E N E V E R made it back to Italy together. Shortly after we returned home from our first trip, the *malocchio* really did seem to take hold of the family. The following years were a blur of funerals. I stood beside the graves of uncles, aunts, dear family friends, and both of my parents.

My father was the last to go. I sometimes think that he cut out prematurely because he just couldn't bear the thought of attending one more funeral, of burying one more loved one.

And, despite the fact that during those years I had begun to build my own family, it wasn't any easier on me.

I married the goofy, WASPy, preppie jock. We eloped actually, right after our first year of college, right after I returned from Italy. It was all very *Romeo and Juliet,* but without the poison.

Our families never came together. The cultural gulf was far too deep. And that caused a great deal of sadness over the course of our many years together.

That sorrow was offset by the fact that we had a son and a daughter and more than our fair share of happiness along the way too.

But when my father died, I felt my roots begin to wither. He had been the last of the generation before me. And now they were all gone. My past seemed nothing more than a faraway dream.

Every day I wondered about my own identity. I was shaky, teetering; without my roots, I knew that I had to fall.

Even my husband and our two children could not keep me grounded.

I'd learned far too well from far too many black-dressed *nonna*s at far too many funerals that what I was supposed to do was beat my breast as I wailed in agony and tried to throw myself into the ground with the coffin. Metaphorically speaking, that was exactly what I was doing. And, as usual, I was doing it to perfection. I spent countless hours wondering which one of my dearly departed I wanted to be buried next to. I even thought about having one of my parents moved so that I could be planted between them.

I was attached to more dead people than living ones. And the ghosts haunted me day and night. I needed some answers. But the ghosts weren't talking. All I could ever hear was the faraway echo of their laughter. Where would I ever find that kind of joy again?

The answer came to me one sleepless night. I suddenly became possessed by the idea that I had to go to Italy.

Because my husband and I were in no financial position to make such a trip on a whim, I set a target date. My little family would see the turn of the millennium in *La Città Eterna*—"The Eternal City," Rome. And whatever it took, it was going to be first-class all the way, the trip of a lifetime.

We saved our money. And I signed up for classes in Italian.

It had been over twenty years since I'd studied it in college, but the language was like an old beloved melody to me, joyful to the ear, and easy to hum along with. I went into the study with my goals set very low; I wanted only to be able to find a bathroom, get a good meal, and ask for directions. But in the joyful environment of adult education, I managed to learn so much more.

We arrived in Italy on December 24, 1999. Christmas Eve. While I had hoped that this would be a trip of discovery for me, or more appropriately, recovery of some intangible something I had lost, I had no desire to retrace the steps of my very first trip. So we got off the plane in Fiumicino airport, picked up our rented car, and bypassed Rome completely.

We spent our first night in the little hillside town of Tivoli, the summer retreat of the Emperor Hadrian. Despite the fact that we'd all been awake for days, with our adrenaline pumping, we had decided unanimously that there was no time for rest. We toured Hadrian's Villa and nearby Villa d'Este, the palatial residence of Cardinal Ippolito d'Este, son of the infamous Lucrezia Borgia.

That evening, we had the traditional all-fish-Christmas-Eve dinner including the eel in a little restaurant in town that had no more than a dozen tables. The waiter spoke not one word of English and begged me to convey his apologies to my family for his lack of social graces. My husband and children had me relate back to him the message that in his country, it was they who regretted not being able to communicate in his language.

At the end of the meal, he brought a platter full of delicate pastries. It was his gift to us and with it he wished us a *Buon Natale*—Merry Christmas. It was indeed.

We spent the night at a little inn right on the grounds of Hadrian's Villa. For people trained to be excited at the thought that "George Washington slept here," the idea of closing one's eyes in a place with thousands of years of history was simply overwhelming. In a strange bed, in a strange country, I slept more soundly than I ever had before. It may have been utter exhaustion that overtook me, but I prefer to believe that there was something magical in the air.

On Christmas Day we left Tivoli and drove south to Sorrento. Our thinking was that nothing would be open anyway and that the best way to spend the day was to enjoy the countryside. We'd been assured that we would be able to find food along the way, that there were twenty-four-hour rest stops along the autostrada, just as there were along American highways. What was surprising though was that the food in Italian pit stops was far superior to what is served in many five-star "Italian" restaurants here, and at one-tenth the cost.

We drove up to Montecassino to see the rebuilt monastery, the original having been destroyed in the infamous World War II battle. The panoramic view made it easy to understand why that hilltop had been a military stronghold—and a place of religious solitude and reflection.

Farther south, we went to the top of Mount Vesuvius. With the exception of a British family on holiday who were also meandering about aimlessly on Christmas Day, the place was deserted. It was an eerie feeling to be standing at the mouth of an active volcano, and we couldn't help but imagine what would happen if it suddenly decided to blow right then and there, as it had so many times before. But all fear was dispelled by the great beauty of the place.

This was punctuated for us quite clearly on our drive down the mountain. On an ancient stone retaining wall, we caught sight of some graffiti we hadn't noticed on the way up. It was written in English, but clearly not by an English-speaking vandal. The graffiti read, "You look Naples!" First we laughed. Then as we rounded the corner we understood the graffiti writer's enthusiasm. The view was so breathtaking we were forced to heed his words and stop the car and simply look. From our vantage point on the side of Vesuvius, we looked down on the city of Naples and all its outlying little towns, out past Sorrento, across the azure blue Mediterranean to the Isle of Capri and beyond.

Somewhere along that coastline was my grandfather's town of Castellammare di Stabia, and we were all anxious to get there before darkness fell. That desire may have been the only thing that got us going again.

The town hadn't changed one iota since my first visit. Even on Christmas Day, the same carnival seemed to be in full swing. We would have liked to have stopped to join in, but there wasn't time. Daylight was quickly fading, and we had to get to our hotel in Sorrento in time to have a proper Christmas dinner. So we drove slowly through the town, soaking in the atmosphere as best we could. Serendipitously, we passed a business with a sign out front that read CASCONE, my grandfather's surname. I wondered if they were relatives and hoped that someday I would be able to come back and find out.

By the time we drove out of town, I was teary-eyed, lost in a wave of nostalgia and longing for loved ones who were long since gone. I was, in fact, just a hairsbreadth away from the wailing and breast-beating when something jolted me back to the present.

Our rented car began jerking, and sputtering, and threatening to . . .

We coasted through a long, dark tunnel before my husband managed to pull the car off to the side of the road, wherein it promptly died. It was well and truly dead. Turning the key in the ignition and pumping the gas pedal was all to no avail; it produced nothing, not even the sound of a last gasp of life. It was over. We were stuck in the middle of nowhere, in a foreign country, in the dark, on Christmas night.

Malocchio, malocchio, malocchio!

My family just wasn't meant to win. Not anywhere. Not ever.

While I was busy working myself into a spectacularly dramatic hysterical lather, and bringing my children right along with me, my husband opted to retreat into his cool, WASPy logic. He remembered having seen a little place—a pizzeria, he thought—just on the other side of the tunnel, and he remembered seeing that the lights were on. He decided that the thing to do was for him and me to walk back there and try to find help. Our children—a twenty-four-year-old son and a twenty-year-old daughter—would stay with the car and watch over our belongings.

Leave my children in the middle of nowhere, in a foreign country, in the dark, on Christmas night? Never!

But as he was the only one who could lead us to the place, and I was the only one who could speak Italian with any degree of proficiency, our options were severely limited. So off we went, through the dark tunnel and back up the hill toward a little shop where the lights were indeed turned on.

I was shocked to find the place open for business, and grateful beyond words. As we walked through the door, the smells of baking bread and garlic nearly dropped me to my knees. Even in a crisis those aromas were irresistible to me.

"Buona sera," the gentleman behind the counter said, welcoming us to his charming establishment.

"*Buona sera*," I replied, wishing that I were there to order some of the beautiful sandwiches and pastries he'd been busily arranging in his glass display case. But I was not. I had a problem. A big problem. And I told him so. "*Abbiamo un gran problema!*"

"*Sì?*" he invited me to tell him. Did I detect a hint of excitement in his voice? It had always, after all, been my experience that Italians love to become involved in big problems.

I certainly didn't want to let him down. But as I wondered where to begin, I realized that I was so upset that I was incapable of finding the right words in English, much less in Italian. All I could manage to tell him was, "*La nostra macchina è morta!*"—"Our car is dead!" Of course I made all the appropriate hand gestures to demonstrate just how dire our circumstances were.

His reaction was perfect. He laughed.

It was my father's laugh, the "I'm not laughing at you" laugh. It was a gentle laugh, a laugh that meant only "Isn't life funny?"

There was only one appropriate response. I began to laugh too—at myself, at my predicament, and at life in general.

Then I went on to explain. I had to struggle through in Italian, since he spoke not one word of English. Even his Italian was difficult for me to understand because he spoke in a heavy southern dialect. But he understood me perfectly, and it didn't take him long to get the situation well in hand. He called our hotel and arranged for them to send a car to pick us up. Then he invited us to sit down and have a cup of espresso to calm our nerves while we waited for help to arrive.

While I have never viewed highly concentrated doses of caffeine as the perfect antidote to feelings of anxiety, I knew that it would be an unforgivable breach of protocol to refuse the offer.

We were invited into the kitchen, where two other gentle-men were hard at work baking breads in the wood-burning oven and slicing meats for the mountain of sandwiches they were preparing.

These two were quite a pair. One was a big, husky guy, the other short and skinny. Both were dressed in white pants, white shirts, and white aprons, as was their boss. But, unlike the boss, they both had little white caps perched at odd angles atop their heads. They were so like Laurel and Hardy that I couldn't look at them for very long for fear that, with my nerves as frayed as they were, my self-control would give out and I would collapse into hysterical laughter.

All three men had cigarettes dangling from the sides of their mouths.

In the corner of the room, a German shepherd was curled up sound asleep.

I was pretty sure that any inspector from any board of health in the United States would have closed them down in an instant. But I was quite certain that the quality of the food was at least as good, and probably better, than anyplace I have ever eaten that had a certificate in the window from some public au-thority guaranteeing my safety.

I did not waver in that opinion even after the baker disposed of his empty cigarette carton by tossing it into the oven with his breads.

While the boss man put on the pot for espresso, my hus-band had me explain to the group in Italian that he was going to go back to the car to wait with our children and that I would stay there with them to wait for the car from the hotel.

They all seemed to think that was a fine idea.

But shortly after my husband left, things began to go awry.

An argument broke out among the three men in the kitchen. Because they were all speaking so quickly and in such a heavy dialect, I couldn't understand what it was all about. But I did pick up enough words to figure out that it had something to do with me. And despite the fact that all three of them kept smiling at me intermittently, I was beginning to get pretty nervous, especially when the dog woke up and started to whine.

I quietly sipped my espresso, struggling to understand what was going on and at the same time planning my escape.

But then, as suddenly as it had begun, the argument ended with hands raised in the air in surrender or triumph, the alpha male standing tall while the other two skulked out the door.

The American part of my brain continued to flash the message that I should still be very worried. But the Italian part told me that somehow everything was okay.

"*Tutto è bene,*" the *padrone* said, assuring me that I should follow my Italian inclination. "Everything's fine," he'd told me. Then he went on to explain that he'd sent his *compari,* his buddies, his pals, his "goombas," to tow our rented car back to his parking lot, where it would be safe for the night.

I watched out the window as the two of them continued to argue in the parking lot. I saw them toss some rope into the back of a little white delivery truck that looked as though it had been borrowed from the Ringling Brothers and Barnum & Bailey Circus. And it was with no small degree of consternation that I realized they were off to "rescue" my family.

I tossed the rest of my espresso back in one gulp. It did not help.

In an effort to distract myself from the many problems at hand, I decided to try to make small talk. I asked why such a place as his was open on Christmas night.

He took great pleasure in explaining it to me. After all the feasting that takes place on Christmas Eve and Christmas Day, people are anxious to get out for a bit of exercise and socializing on Christmas night. But sooner or later, they will get hungry again—not for a big meal, but for a snack. So little sandwich shops like his did remarkable business. It was, in fact, his most profitable night of the year. He was open for business from five o'clock in the evening until five o'clock the following morning. And by the time he closed, he told me, every single sandwich would be gone.

Fortunately, the next day was also a holiday. It was Saint Stefano's Day. He couldn't tell me exactly who Saint Stefano was or why he deserved a holiday. And no one else I asked over the next few days could either. But I understood perfectly. It didn't really matter what name was attached to it, the day after Christmas had been rightfully designated a day of rest, not just for the privileged few, but also for everybody.

While I was busy learning the mores and customs of the land, and enjoying every minute of it, my family was busy dealing with more practical matters.

When the rescue team of Laurel and Hardy appeared on the scene, my children were terrified that their little circus-mobile was the car that had been sent to transport us to our supposedly luxurious hotel in Sorrento. My husband only exacerbated the situation by happily announcing, "Look, it's the guys!"

They jumped out of their little truck like the superheroes they were and went right to the job at hand. There was much debating—in Italian, of course—furious gesticulating, and non-stop smoking.

It was the smoking that made my family so nervous, not only because of all the proven health hazards, but also because they'd noticed that the car was leaking gasoline at an alarming rate. How could they convey that to the rescue team?

The answer was obvious. Just say the word and add a vowel

to the end of it. "Gasoline-a!" they all shouted in unison, pointing to the puddle that was spreading beneath the car.

It worked. They got their point across. And after a silent
movie–type slap-off, both cigarettes were tossed well out of the
danger zone.

Further antics ensued with regard to the actual towing of
the car. But before long, everyone had returned to the sandwich
shop safe and sound.

Another round of espresso was served, on the house, of
course. And a sleek Mercedes limousine arrived to bring us to
our hotel.

When my husband tried to show our appreciation by offer-
ing a small gratuity for all the trouble these gentlemen had gone
to on our account, pandemonium erupted more dramatically
than Vesuvius ever had. They refused to take our money. It was
unthinkable. It was Christmas after all, and they'd only done
what was right, what they would have done for anyone in our
situation.

I begged. I pleaded. I told them we would not leave otherwise. They knew I meant business. They understood women
like me. So in the end, they acquiesced. After just the right
amount of drama, they accepted our thanks graciously. And we
parted with the warmest wishes for a Merry Christmas and a
Happy New Year.

From what seemed a disaster at the outset, came an experience I wouldn't trade for all the world.

In a single day—the last Christmas Day of the millennium—
we'd seen snow at the top of Vesuvius and flowers blooming in
Sorrento. We'd endured what originally seemed to be an
unimaginable crisis and were miraculously rescued. And at the
end of it all, we enjoyed the most lavish dinner we may ever
have, in one of the most picturesque places in the world. It was
a Christmas that I doubt we will ever top.

But our journey had just barely begun.

There was still the glory of Rome and a new millennium to celebrate.

After a few wonderful days in the south, touring Pompeii, Herculaneum, and the Amalfi Coast, we were back on the road, headed toward our ultimate destination, the city into which all roads lead: Rome.

We hadn't made any specific plans for New Year's Eve. We'd decided that we would figure out what to do once we got there. When we asked the concierge of the hotel for suggestions, he recommended a neighborhood restaurant that he assured us would be perfect for the occasion.

My husband and son volunteered to go and check it out. And I gratefully allowed them to do it, since I was tired and welcomed a rest, and since we were told that there was someone there who was quite proficient in English.

As it turned out, however, the English "expert" could say little more than "Hello. How are you? Welcome to our restaurant." Beyond that, they were all quite lost. But because the concierge had called ahead to ask for reservations for New Year's Eve in our name, they all somehow came to the understanding that my husband would like to see a menu. And it was with a great deal of pride that one was proffered.

It was a special menu, planned with great care for the evening's festivities. A banquet of eight sumptuous courses would be served beginning at eight o'clock in the evening and continuing on into the wee hours of the morning. It seemed to be just what we wanted, and my husband confirmed the reservation on the spot. He had just one small question. There was one word on the menu that he did not recognize. *Anatra*. *"Che cos'è?"* he asked, using one of the few phrases he knew in Italian as he pointed to the word. "What is that?"

"Anatra." The English "expert" read it aloud for him.

"*Non capisco,*" my husband told him. "I don't understand. What is it in English?"

The problem was clear. The "expert" thought for a moment, then resorted to the first remedy that every person faced with a language barrier tries to employ. "Ah-nah-tra," he repeated, more loudly and slowly than he had before.

My husband shook his head and shrugged his shoulders to display his continued lack of understanding.

"Aaah-nah-tra," the "expert" said, trying to clarify.

They went back and forth like that for a while until the "expert" realized the hopelessness of the situation. He thought for a moment and discovered the answer. "Anatra," he said one more time. Then he put his hand to his face, moved it like a duck's bill, and said, "Quack! Quack!"

The duck was delicious. As were all of the other dishes that were served to us during this last evening of the year. The restaurant was full of local people—couples, families, parties of friends. We were the only foreigners. And as such, we had no idea what to expect. It was part of the excitement.

While the ball was set to drop in Times Square, and Big Ben would chime in London at the stroke of midnight, and lavish celebrations were taking place in every major city in the world, we were a little disconcerted to notice that the place in which we had chosen to ring in the millennium didn't even have a clock in evidence.

We were even more disconcerted when people began leaving the restaurant at about a quarter to twelve. Where were they going? we wondered. What should we do?

Follow them, we decided. So we quickly paid our check and headed out into the streets, which we discovered was where the real party was taking place. But we were less than ten minutes away from the New Year, and we had no champagne with which to toast it. That problem was quickly solved when we noticed that street vendors were everywhere, selling bottles of champagne for just a few thousand lire. Of course there were no glasses to be had, but that didn't seem to be bothering any of the other people who were holding on to bottles just waiting for the appropriate moment to pop the cork.

But how would we know when the moment had arrived? There was no ball, no clock, no one to officiate the countdown.

Before we knew it, someone in the crowd shouted, *"Buon Millennio!"* and popped the cork on his champagne bottle. Other people began to look at their watches and decide that it did indeed look like midnight had arrived. We were in a new millennium. Corks popped. Champagne spilled. And everyone was wishing everyone else a *"Buon Millennio!"*

Fireworks began to appear in the sky, and suddenly, without any pomp and circumstance—only joy and laughter and dancing in the streets—we found ourselves in a new millennium. In the land of "no rules," we didn't all pop our corks at once, but we all got there just the same.

For me, it was a dream come true.

The party went on until dawn, and we would liked to have stayed until the last champagne bottle was emptied. But we retired not long after midnight. With just a few days left in the city, we still had so much to see.

Somehow in two weeks' time we did it all. We hit all the major points of interest and some little out-of-the-way places as well.

On our last night, we returned to one of those little out-of-the-way places for our farewell dinner. We had long since learned that the best way to order in a neighborhood restaurant was to give the waiter a general idea of what you were in the mood to eat—fish, meat, fowl—and then let him decide what you ought to have.

That night, I was in the mood for fish, always a good choice along a Mediterranean coastline. Our waiter, Fulvio, heartily approved of my good judgment and promptly headed over to an ice-covered counter that ran along one wall where fresh, whole fish were laid out on display. He thought it over carefully, then picked one up by the tail and smiled as he wiggled it in the air, awaiting my nod of approval. Only then did he bring the fish back into the kitchen to be cooked.

That night we ate as though we might never do so again. We knew that it would certainly be a long time before we had food as fresh and as lovingly prepared as we had enjoyed during our two-week sojourn there. We ordered antipasto, pasta, entrées, insalata, and even dessert. And we sat for hours as we savored every delicious bite.

And in the end, when we were sure we could not swallow another thing, Fulvio brought us one last treat.

This is the most treasured recipe I have in my personal files. It is one that I have never actually made with my own two hands. But I will someday. And when I do, it will go down in my life's logbook as yet another dream come true.

Limoncello

Step 1: No more Chianti! By the time they've put the limoncello on the table, you've already had more than enough.

Step 2: Get six big lemons from Sorrento.

Do you see the problem? Fulvio did not. And a lifetime of experience with Italian men had taught me that it was futile to even try to explain it to him. So I simply smiled and nodded and took down his recipe as though I would be using it as soon as I got back to my own little kitchen in New York. I hope that in the end the joke will be on me. And I promise that I will be the first to laugh if ever I am in the position to concoct this lovely brew. It would mean, of course, that I had a kitchen—presumably attached to a really nice house—somewhere along the Bay of Naples or the Amalfi coast, close enough to Sorrento to be able to get those beautiful lemons. They are as big as softballs, with a sweet fragrance that makes our "lemony fresh" products here smell like toxic waste in comparison.

> Step 3: Peel the lemons gently, taking only the best of the zest. Put the peelings into a large jar.
>
> Step 4: Add a kilogram, which is a little over two pounds, of sugar.
>
> Step 5: Pour in a liter of pure grain alcohol.
>
> Step 6: Let stand for six weeks on your kitchen counter to bask in the Italian sun.
>
> Step 7: Strain. And *voilà,* you have limoncello.

You can find it in liquor stores here. But it's not the same thing. Not even close. What's in those bottles marked "limoncello" is a syrupy substance that is far too sweet. And most of it is about as "lemony fresh" as furniture polish. The fact that it may say "Made in Italy" on the bottle doesn't guarantee anything.

The only proper limoncello comes in unmarked bottles.

What's inside has not been produced in a factory or been inspected by any federal agency. It has the crisp, clean taste of freshly squeezed lemonade. It also has the knockout punch of a heavyweight champion.

At most *trattorie*—family-style restaurants in Italy—a bottle of limoncello is proffered after the meal as a nicety. It is unwise to assume that this is an invitation to finish off the bottle. It is, in fact, unwise to have more than one or two shots. It's not that the *padrone* of the restaurant would take offense. He might even be somewhat amused, particularly if he knows that you are a foreigner. It is unwise because, as good as it tastes, and as lovely an afterglow as it produces, it has about the same effect on the human body as drinking battery acid.

Do not, however, let this deter you from enjoying a little nip. While it may be unwise to drink too much limoncello, it is completely unacceptable to refuse it.

My daughter committed the ultimate faux pas of trying to graciously decline Fulvio's offer of an after-dinner *digestivo*, namely limoncello. To my great surprise, he did not protest. He simply left the table and returned moments later with a small dish of what he tried to pass off as lemon sorbet. It took only one small taste for my daughter to realize what it really was, frozen limoncello. She and Fulvio exchanged knowing looks, and with a smile, she conceded defeat. Under Fulvio's watchful eye, she proceeded to ingest her *digestivo*.

At our very last dinner, on our very last night in Italy, we realized that perhaps there were some rules that couldn't be broken.

The next morning, as we waited to board the plane at Fiumicino airport for our long journey home, we were all in tears. It had been a vacation that had exceeded all of our expectations, and none of us wanted to see it come to an end. But more than that, there was an overwhelming sense that we should stay—forever. The Roman air had worked its magic on us like pixie dust. Just as Peter Pan could not escape the lure of Never-Never Land, the Eternal City had taken captive our souls.

But we were still Americans first. And the "no rules" rule could not override the duty-bound attitudes that had been instilled in us over the course of a lifetime. There were jobs to return to, school for my daughter, a mortgage to pay, family, friends, and even pets awaiting our homecoming. So we boarded the plane in spite of ourselves, laden with gifts and personal treasures, and a solemn vow to return.

The night before, each of us had tossed our three coins into the fountain. I'd also tossed in three coins that I'd taken from my father's pocket on the day he died. Symbolically, at least, I'd brought him back.

The trip was a raging success, not only because of the joy I'd shared with my family—a joy we will all carry in our hearts for the rest of our lives—but also because I'd found what I was looking for. I found it not far from the very place where my grandfather had been born over a hundred years before.

A few miles north of Castellammare di Stabia is a little town called Stabia at the base of Mount Vesuvius. Stabia has been destroyed by the volcano seven times. And seven times the people went back and rebuilt. On the surface, that seems utterly insane. But in the grand scheme of things, it is as pragmatic a way of dealing with life as any other.

You can buy insurance policies, get regular checkups, avoid fat, eat fiber, and wear a gas mask. But those are only psychological Band-Aids. You don't have to live at the base of a volcano to understand that life is risky business. There are no guarantees. Even insurance policies are loaded with fine print.

I have learned that the best we can do is live with a passion. Dance at the foot of the volcano. Eat. Drink. Laugh. Love. And be grateful for every precious moment. That is the secret of happiness.

I have not yet mastered the art, but I am proud to say that there is something in my blood that keeps me trying.

GINA CASCONE was born and raised in central New Jersey. *Pagan Babies* (1982) was her first book, soon followed by *Mother's Little Helper* (1984). In 1985, she began writing with her sister Annette under the pseudonym A. G. Cascone. The team produced more than twenty humor books, teen thrillers, and humorous spine tinglers for middle-grade readers. From 1989 to 1995, Gina and her husband owned Wit and Wisdom Booksellers, an independent bookstore in Lawrenceville, New Jersey. The mother of two children, Gina lives with her husband in New York City.

Printed in the United States
By Bookmasters